Compose Key Sequence
Reference Guide 2012

Compose Key Sequence
Reference Guide 2012

Sander van Geloven

Hellebaard
ICT Analysis, Design and Management

Published globally on-line by Hellebaard
Utrecht, Netherlands
http://hellebaard.nl

Design and textual material copyright © 2012 Sander van Geloven
Utrecht, Netherlands
http://hellebaard.nl

UTF-8 (Unicode) compose sequence © 2012 X.Org Foundation
Delaware, United States
http://xorg.freedesktop.org
X11 License
Retrieved on the 12th of August 2012 from libX11 1.5
http://cgit.freedesktop.org/xorg/lib/libX11/tree/nls/en_US.UTF-8/Compose.pre

ISBN 978-1-4681-4110-8 perfect bound paperback in English

Content was typeset in LATEX and cover was designed in Inkscape
Typefaces used are GNU FreeFont family revision 2304, Linux Biolinum Keyboard and Droid Sans

Printed at a CreateSpace print-on-demand location

First edition 2012

To all novice and experienced users
of GNOME, Unity, KDE and X11
in the hope that you can enter
a wider range of characters
in a more efficient way.

Contents

Contents

Chapter 1
Introduction

This is a reference guide of contemporary compose key sequences offered by GNOME, Unity, KDE and other X11-based desktop environments. Below, an introduction to compose key sequences is given. This is followed by several chapters providing different practical overviews of compose key sequences.

1.1   Writing on a computer

Computers are used more and more for writing texts. Creating *any* element of all known written languages is relatively easy with a pen or pencil. Entering exotic characters via a keyboard into a computer might prove to be extremely difficult. Most external keyboards offer a little over one hundred keys and laptops or external mini keyboards offer a little over eighty keys. Because of limited space on a keyboard there exist a variety of keyboard layouts which are optimized for specific languages. Each keyboard layout allows users to enter characters in terms of letters, numerals, diacritics, ligatures, punctuation marks, currency signs and basic mathematical symbols, but only for the languages it supports.

See for example the [Q][W][E][R][T][Z] keyboards used in Germany, Austria and Switzerland with additional keys for vowels with diacritics such as [Ö] and [Ü]. On [Q][W][E][R][T][Y] keyboards, these keys are hard, if not impossible, to be found. More obviously, both types of keyboard layouts have interchanged the location of [Y] and [Z] to facilitate the use of these letters in the German language. Similar differences are found on [A][Z][E][R][T][Y] keyboards designed for French speaking countries.

A variety of mechanisms exist to extend the range of characters which can be entered beyond the number of physical keys on the keyboard. Laptops and mini keyboards usually have a Function hardware modifier key [Fn] to assign a second character to a key to make up for the difference of nearly twenty missing keys compared to a standard external keyboard. The hardware modifier key could also assign multimedia functions to keys, whereas on external keyboards these are usually additional keys.

The range is further extended with well known modifier keys such as [⇧] or Shift keys. Other well known modifier keys are [Ctrl] and [Alt] for conveying shortcuts to the desktop environment such as copy and paste commands. However most shortcuts manipulate the appearance of windows or trigger application specific functionality and cannot extend the range of supported characters. A limited range is a problem when frequently using diacritics, ligatures such as [æ] and [ß], punctuation marks such as [«] and [»] and symbols such as [°] and [±] which are not to be found on the keyboard at hand. Hence, writing in multiple languages demanding different keyboard layouts can be difficult or time consuming.

1.2   Alternative ways of entering characters

At the moment, most computers store characters in Unicode. This is a character encoding that has been developed to represent elements of almost any written language and currently supports more than 110,000 characters. To be able to enter these characters it is possible to browse, copy and paste them using websites such as Unicode Lookup and FileFormat.Info or the GNOME Character Map application. Each Unicode character has an unique identifier which is a hexadecimal value of up to five positions consisting of the numerals 0 to 9 or the letters A to F. Usually a prefix is added explicitly refer to a Unicode such as `uni017E`, `U+017E` or, as used in this reference guide, `U017E`. When known, it is possible to enter Unicode directly after pressing `Ctrl`+`⇧`+`U`. If subsequently `1` `7` `E` `⏎` is pressed, the leading zeros can be omitted, a ž will be the result. This is useful if `ž` is not available on the keyboard. Nevertheless, this is not an efficient way to use regularly because the hexadecimal codes are *somewhat* hard to remember.

Alternative ways to enter characters involve the modifier keys Alternate Graphics key `AltGr` and dead keys. Dead keys such as `'`, `"`, `` ` ``, `´`, `~` and `^` or `˘` plus a letter typically attach a diacritic to a letter. For ergonomic reasons I would not endorse using the `AltGr`. It disturbs the identical functionality offered by two `Alt` keys which are symmetrically placed on both sides of the keyboard and often used in combination with matching `Ctrl` keys. Secondly, `AltGr` has to be pressed simultaneously with `⇧` or other keys. In an effort to document `AltGr` a few extra symbols have been crammed unappealingly on most keyboards. Dead keys are especially counter productive when using single or double quotes regularly, as software developers do. One can spend a lot of time escaping the dead keys with space bar `⎵` which breaks the flow while typing. Furthermore the number of combinations with dead keys is limited making it difficult to create Å, ū or Ž on certain keyboards.

1.3   Compose key sequences

Other character encodings predating Unicode had similar problems. Alternative methods have therefore been developed for entering characters that are hard to find on keyboard layouts. One of these is the use of compose key sequences which is the topic of this reference guide. A Compose key is a special kind of modifier key. It signals that the following predefined sequence of two or more keystrokes should be interpreted as a Unicode character, as is illustrated by the following examples. Pressing, and releasing, Compose followed by `O` and then `E` produces the ligature Œ. When Compose is followed by `a` and `` ` `` or by `` ` `` and `a` the letter a with grave accent à is generated. A copyright symbol © will appear when Compose is followed by `o` and `c`. Clearly, the advantage of compose key sequences is that the sequences are easy to deduce and to remember. This is because they describe the visual form of the character produced. Incidentally, the compose key functions independently of language input methods.

Note that an explicitly designated Compose key is very rarely available on present day keyboards, however it is possible to assign a non-functional key to take on the role of Compose key. The Windows logo key `⊞` on Microsoft compatible keyboards is used for shortcuts by Microsoft Windows. For example `⊞`+`D` will minimize all windows and show the desktop or restore the windows and `⊞`+`L` will lock the screen. In GNOME, KDE, etc. the same is achieved with the key combinations `Ctrl`+`Alt`+`D` and `Ctrl`+`Alt`+`L`. Actually, GNOME, KDE, etc. have no specific use for `⊞` rendering it a generic dead key and at the same time making it a perfect candidate for a Compose key.

Similarly Apple compatible keyboards have the Command key `⌘` for shortcuts in Max OS X. For example `⌘`+`M` minimizes the active window. When assigning in GNOME, KDE, etc. `⊞` or `⌘` as Compose key, please do this for both the left and right key promoting ergonomic keyboard usage. To be vendor independent, this reference guide uses `⊡` for the Compose key.

Both the Menu key `▤` and Option key `⌥` are usually reserved to launch a context menu, exactly as the right mouse button does. This functionality is also supported in GNOME, KDE, etc. and therefore these keys are no suitable candidates as compose key.

I would like to thank Stevan White for his work on the GNU FreeFont family which is used extensively in this guide. Hopefully my efforts have paid off presenting compose key sequences developed by the X.Org and GNOME communities. I, the author, am not liable for any direct or indirect damages caused as a result of using the information contained in this publication or this publication as physical object.

Having said this, I conclude by wishing you a more efficient way of entering characters by means of compose key sequences which are found in this reference guide.

Sander van Geloven
Utrecht, the Netherlands, September 2012

Chapter 2
Unicode Compose Sequences Overview

At the time of writing over 4,000 compose key sequences have been defined in the X.Org project. Even when sequences using dead keys and certain non-western scripts are excluded, still approximately 2,800 compose key sequences remain. This chapter offers a detailed overview of these.

The compose key sequences listed here are grouped in sections. Each section holds compose key sequences resulting in Unicode characters of a certain Unicode general category. The first section is on lowercase letters and the second on upper case letters, which is followed by sections on other general categories concerning letters. Then several sections follow on general categories on punctuation, numbers, symbols and finally some special general categories. The compose key sequences in each section are sorted by their Unicode identifier which is listed on the left in the first column. This results in reasonably practical ordering of these characters as they have been defined by the Unicode Consortium.

Not all fonts can represent certain letters, especially symbols, in an unambiguous way. Where possible, each Unicode character is therefore shown in the serif, sans-serif and monospaced fonts of the GNU FreeFont family in the second column.

All compose sequences resulting in the character shown on the left side of the overview are listed in the third column of the overview, one below the other. The numbers 1 to 4 indicate the order of the keys that need to be pressed subsequently in order to enter the compose sequence. A minimum of two keys is always needed. The official Unicode name of the character is listed on the right in the fourth column.

For practical reasons this reference guide has excluded compose key sequences for Hangul, Tamil, Japanese, Myanmar, Telugu and Tibetan scripts and sequences using dead keys. It does document extensively compose key sequences for Latin, Greek, Cyrillic, and many other scripts as well as mathematical symbols, currency signs and punctuation marks. These make up the majority of the several thousands of defined compose key sequences.

The last section of this chapter contains combining diacritics. This is not an official general category according to Unicode but has been added here to represent remaining compose key sequences that result in two Unicode characters instead of a single character. The latter character of these two is always a combining diacritical mark, effectively resulting in the appearance of a single character.

2.1 Letter, Lowercase (Ll)

Unicode	Character			1 2 3 4	Name
U00B5	µ	µ	µ	/u mu u/	Micro sign
U00DF	ß	ß	ß	ss	Latin small letter sharp s
U00E0	à	à	à	`a a`	Latin small letter a with grave
U00E1	á	á	á	'a a' a´ ´a	Latin small letter a with acute
U00E2	â	â	â	>a ^a a> a^	Latin small letter a with circumflex
U00E3	ã	ã	ã	a~ ~a	Latin small letter a with tilde
U00E4	ä	ä	ä	"a a" a¨ ¨a	Latin small letter a with diaeresis
U00E5	å	å	å	*a a* aa oa	Latin small letter a with ring above
U00E6	æ	æ	æ	ae	Latin small letter ae
U00E7	ç	ç	ç	,c c, ¸c	Latin small letter c with cedilla
U00E8	è	è	è	`e e`	Latin small letter e with grave
U00E9	é	é	é	'e e' e´ ´e	Latin small letter e with acute
U00EA	ê	ê	ê	>e ^e e> e^	Latin small letter e with circumflex
U00EB	ë	ë	ë	"e e" e¨ ¨e	Latin small letter e with diaeresis
U00EC	ì	ì	ì	`i i`	Latin small letter i with grave
U00ED	í	í	í	'i i' i´ ´i	Latin small letter i with acute

Unicode	Character			1 2 3 4	Name
U00EE	î	î	î	>i	Latin small letter i with circumflex
				^i	
				i>	
				i^	
U00EF	ï	ï	ï	"i	Latin small letter i with diaeresis
				i"	
				i¨	
				¨i	
U00F0	ð	ð	ð	dh	Latin small letter eth
U00F1	ñ	ñ	ñ	n~	Latin small letter n with tilde
				~n	
U00F2	ò	ò	ò	`o	Latin small letter o with grave
				o`	
U00F3	ó	ó	ó	'o	Latin small letter o with acute
				o'	
				o´	
				´o	
U00F4	ô	ô	ô	>o	Latin small letter o with circumflex
				^o	
				o>	
				o^	
U00F5	õ	õ	õ	o~	Latin small letter o with tilde
				~o	
U00F6	ö	ö	ö	"o	Latin small letter o with diaeresis
				o"	
				o¨	
				¨o	
U00F8	ø	ø	ø	/o	Latin small letter o with stroke
				o/	
U00F9	ù	ù	ù	`u	Latin small letter u with grave
				u`	
U00FA	ú	ú	ú	'u	Latin small letter u with acute
				u'	
				u´	
				´u	
U00FB	û	û	û	>u	Latin small letter u with circumflex
				^u	
				u>	
				u^	
U00FC	ü	ü	ü	"u	Latin small letter u with diaeresis
				u"	
				u¨	
				¨u	
U00FD	ý	ý	ý	'y	Latin small letter y with acute
				y'	
				y´	
				´y	
U00FE	þ	þ	þ	th	Latin small letter thorn
U00FF	ÿ	ÿ	ÿ	"y	Latin small letter y with diaeresis
				y"	
				y¨	
				¨y	

Unicode	Character			1 2 3 4	Name
U0101	ā	ā	ā	_a a_ ¯a	Latin small letter a with macron
U0103	ă	ă	ă	Ua a (ba	Latin small letter a with breve
U0105	ą	ą	ą	,a ;a a,	Latin small letter a with ogonek
U0107	ć	ć	ć	'c c' ´c	Latin small letter c with acute
U0109	ĉ	ĉ	ĉ	^c	Latin small letter c with circumflex
U010B	ċ	ċ	ċ	.c c.	Latin small letter c with dot above
U010D	č	č	č	<c c< cc	Latin small letter c with caron
U010F	ď	ď	ď	<d cd d<	Latin small letter d with caron
U0111	đ	đ	đ	-d /d d-	Latin small letter d with stroke
U0113	ē	ē	ē	-e _e e- e_ ¯e	Latin small letter e with macron
U0115	ĕ	ĕ	ĕ	Ue be	Latin small letter e with breve
U0117	ė	ė	ė	.e e.	Latin small letter e with dot above
U0119	ę	ę	ę	,e ;e e,	Latin small letter e with ogonek
U011B	ě	ě	ě	<e ce e<	Latin small letter e with caron
U011D	ĝ	ĝ	ĝ	^g	Latin small letter g with circumflex
U011F	ğ	ğ	ğ	Ug bg g (gU g˘ ˘g	Latin small letter g with breve
U0121	ġ	ġ	ġ	.g g.	Latin small letter g with dot above
U0123	ġ	ġ	ġ	,g g, .g	Latin small letter g with cedilla

Unicode	Character	1 2 3 4	Name
U0125	ĥ ĥ ĥ	^h	Latin small letter h with circumflex
U0127	ħ ħ ħ	/h	Latin small letter h with stroke
U0129	ĩ ĩ ĩ	i~ ~i	Latin small letter i with tilde
U012B	ī ī ī	-i _i i- i_ ¯i	Latin small letter i with macron
U012D	ĭ ĭ ĭ	Ui bi	Latin small letter i with breve
U012F	į į į	,i ;i i, i;	Latin small letter i with ogonek
U0131	ı ı ı	.i i.	Latin small letter dotless i
U0133	ĳ ĳ ĳ	ij	Latin small ligature ij
U0135	ĵ ĵ ĵ	^j	Latin small letter j with circumflex
U0137	ķ ķ ķ	,k k, ˛k	Latin small letter k with cedilla
U0138	ĸ ĸ ĸ	kk	Latin small letter kra
U013A	ĺ ĺ ĺ	'l l' ´l	Latin small letter l with acute
U013C	ļ ļ ļ	,l l, ˛l	Latin small letter l with cedilla
U013E	ľ ľ ľ	<l cl l<	Latin small letter l with caron
U0142	ł ł ł	/l l/	Latin small letter l with stroke
U0144	ń ń ń	'n n' ´n	Latin small letter n with acute
U0146	ņ ņ ņ	,n n, ˛n	Latin small letter n with cedilla
U0148	ň ň ň	<n cn n<	Latin small letter n with caron
U014B	ŋ ŋ ŋ	ng	Latin small letter eng
U014D	ō ō ō	-o _o o- o_ ¯o	Latin small letter o with macron
U014F	ŏ ŏ ŏ	Uo bo	Latin small letter o with breve

Unicode	Character	1 2 3 4	Name
U0151	ő ő ő	=o	Latin small letter o with double acute
U0153	œ œ œ	oe	Latin small ligature oe
U0155	ŕ ŕ ŕ	'r r' ´r	Latin small letter r with acute
U0157	ŗ ŗ ŗ	,r r, ˛r	Latin small letter r with cedilla
U0159	ř ř ř	<r cr r<	Latin small letter r with caron
U015B	ś ś ś	's s' ´s	Latin small letter s with acute
U015D	ŝ ŝ ŝ	^s	Latin small letter s with circumflex
U015F	ş ş ş	,s s, s˛ ˛s	Latin small letter s with cedilla
U0161	š š š	<s cs s<	Latin small letter s with caron
U0163	ţ ţ ţ	,t t, ˛t	Latin small letter t with cedilla
U0165	ť ť ť	<t ct t<	Latin small letter t with caron
U0167	ŧ ŧ ŧ	/t t- t/	Latin small letter t with stroke
U0169	ũ ũ ũ	u~ ~u	Latin small letter u with tilde
U016B	ū ū ū	-u _u u- u_ ¯u	Latin small letter u with macron
U016D	ŭ ŭ ŭ	Uʋ bu uu	Latin small letter u with breve
U016F	ů ů ů	*u ou u*	Latin small letter u with ring above
U0171	ű ű ű	=u	Latin small letter u with double acute
U0173	ų ų ų	,u ;u u,	Latin small letter u with ogonek
U0175	ŵ ŵ ŵ	^w w^	Latin small letter w with circumflex
U0177	ŷ ŷ ŷ	^y y^	Latin small letter y with circumflex

Unicode	Character			1 2 3 4	Name
U017A	ź	ź	ź	'z	Latin small letter z with acute
				z'	
				´z	
U017C	ż	ż	ż	.z	Latin small letter z with dot above
				z.	
U017E	ž	ž	ž	<z	Latin small letter z with caron
				cz	
				vz	
				z<	
U017F	ſ	ſ	ſ	fS	Latin small letter long s
				fs	
U0180	ƀ	ƀ	ƀ	/b	Latin small letter b with stroke
U01A1	ơ	ơ	ơ	+o	Latin small letter o with horn
U01B0	ư	ư	ư	+u	Latin small letter u with horn
U01B6	ƶ	ƶ	ƶ	/z	Latin small letter z with stroke
U01CE	ǎ	ǎ	ǎ	ca	Latin small letter a with caron
U01D0	ǐ	ǐ	ǐ	ci	Latin small letter i with caron
U01D2	ǒ	ǒ	ǒ	co	Latin small letter o with caron
U01D4	ǔ	ǔ	ǔ	cu	Latin small letter u with caron
U01D6	ǖ	ǖ	ǖ	_"u	Latin small letter u with diaeresis and macron
				_ü	
				⁻"u	
				⁻ü	
U01D8	ǘ	ǘ	ǘ	'"u	Latin small letter u with diaeresis and acute
				'ü	
				´"u	
				´ü	
U01DA	ǚ	ǚ	ǚ	c"u	Latin small letter u with diaeresis and caron
				cü	
U01DC	ǜ	ǜ	ǜ	`"u	Latin small letter u with diaeresis and grave
				`ü	
U01DF	ǟ	ǟ	ǟ	_"a	Latin small letter a with diaeresis and macron
				_ä	
				⁻"a	
				⁻ä	
U01E1	ǡ	ǡ	ǡ	_.a	Latin small letter a with dot above and macron
				_ȧ	
				⁻.a	
				⁻ȧ	
U01E3	ǣ	ǣ	ǣ	_æ	Latin small letter ae with macron
				⁻æ	
U01E5	ǥ	ǥ	ǥ	/g	Latin small letter g with stroke
U01E7	ǧ	ǧ	ǧ	cg	Latin small letter g with caron
U01E9	ǩ	ǩ	ǩ	ck	Latin small letter k with caron
U01EB	ǫ	ǫ	ǫ	;o	Latin small letter o with ogonek
U01ED	ǭ	ǭ	ǭ	_;o	Latin small letter o with ogonek and macron
				_ǫ	
				⁻;o	
				⁻ǫ	
U01EF	ǯ	ǯ	ǯ	cʒ	Latin small letter ezh with caron
U01F0	ǰ	ǰ	ǰ	cj	Latin small letter j with caron

Unicode	Character	1 2 3 4	Name
U01F5	ǵ ǵ ǵ	' g ´ g	Latin small letter g with acute
U01F9	ǹ ǹ ǹ	` n	Latin small letter n with grave
U01FB	ǻ ǻ ǻ	' å * ' a ´ å	Latin small letter a with ring above and acute
U01FD	ǽ ǽ ǽ	' æ ´ æ	Latin small letter ae with acute
U01FF	ǿ ǿ ǿ	' / o ' ø ´ / o ´ ø	Latin small letter o with stroke and acute
U021F	ȟ ȟ ȟ	c h	Latin small letter h with caron
U0227	ȧ ȧ ȧ	. a	Latin small letter a with dot above
U0229	ȩ ȩ ȩ	, e	Latin small letter e with cedilla
U022B	ȫ ȫ ȫ	_ " o _ ö ⁻ " o ⁻ ö	Latin small letter o with diaeresis and macron
U022D	ȭ ȭ ȭ	_ ~ o _ õ ⁻ ~ o ⁻ õ	Latin small letter o with tilde and macron
U022F	ȯ ȯ ȯ	. o	Latin small letter o with dot above
U0231	ȱ ȱ ȱ	_ . o _ ȯ ⁻ . o ⁻ ȯ	Latin small letter o with dot above and macron
U0233	ȳ ȳ ȳ	_ y ⁻ y	Latin small letter y with macron
U0259	ə ə ə	e e	Latin small letter schwa
U0268	ɨ ɨ ɨ	/ i	Latin small letter i with stroke
U02A1	ʡ ʡ ʡ	/ ?	Latin letter glottal stop with stroke
U0390	ΐ ΐ ΐ	' " ι ' ϊ ´ " ι ´ ϊ	Greek small letter iota with dialytika and tonos
U03AC	ά ά ά	' α ´ α α '	Greek small letter alpha with tonos
U03AD	έ έ έ	' ε ´ ε ε '	Greek small letter epsilon with tonos
U03AE	ή ή ή	' η ´ η η '	Greek small letter eta with tonos
U03AF	ί ί ί	' ι ´ ι	Greek small letter iota with tonos

Unicode	Character	1 2 3 4	Name

U03B0	ΰ ΰ ΰ	`' "υ`
		`' ϋ`
		`´ "υ`
		`´ ϋ`
			Greek small letter upsilon with dialytika and tonos

U03CA	ϊ ϊ ϊ	`" ι` `ι "`	Greek small letter iota with dialytika
U03CB	ϋ ϋ ϋ	`" υ` `υ "`	Greek small letter upsilon with dialytika

U03CC	ό ό ό	`' ο`
		`´ ο`
		`ο '`
			Greek small letter omicron with tonos

U03CD	ύ ύ ύ	`' υ`
		`´ υ`
		`υ '`
			Greek small letter upsilon with tonos

U03CE	ώ ώ ώ	`' ω`
		`´ ω`
		`ω '`
			Greek small letter omega with tonos

U0439	й й й	`U и` `b и`	Cyrillic small letter short i
U0450	ѐ ѐ ѐ	`` ` e ``	Cyrillic small letter ie with grave
U0451	ё ё ё	`" e`	Cyrillic small letter io
U0453	ѓ ѓ ѓ	`' г` `´ г`	Cyrillic small letter gje
U0457	ї ї ї	`" i`	Cyrillic small letter yi
U045C	ќ ќ ќ	`' v` `´ v`	Cyrillic small letter kje
U045D	ѝ ѝ ѝ	`` ` и ``	Cyrillic small letter i with grave
U045E	ў ў ў	`U y` `b y`	Cyrillic small letter short u
U0493	ғ ғ ғ	`/ г`	Cyrillic small letter ghe with stroke
U049F	ҟ ҟ ҟ	`/ v`	Cyrillic small letter ka with stroke
U04B1	ұ ұ ұ	`/ y`	Cyrillic small letter straight u with stroke
U04C2	҂ ҂ ҂	`U ж` `b ж`	Cyrillic small letter zhe with breve
U04D1	ӑ ӑ ӑ	`U a` `b a`	Cyrillic small letter a with breve
U04D3	ӓ ӓ ӓ	`" a`	Cyrillic small letter a with diaeresis
U04D7	ӗ ӗ ӗ	`U e` `b e`	Cyrillic small letter ie with breve
U04DB	ӛ ӛ ӛ	`" ә`	Cyrillic small letter schwa with diaeresis
U04DD	ӝ ӝ ӝ	`" ж`	Cyrillic small letter zhe with diaeresis
U04DF	ӟ ӟ ӟ	`" з`	Cyrillic small letter ze with diaeresis
U04E3	ӣ ӣ ӣ	`_ и` `¯ и`	Cyrillic small letter i with macron
U04E5	ӥ ӥ ӥ	`" и`	Cyrillic small letter i with diaeresis
U04E7	ӧ ӧ ӧ	`" о`	Cyrillic small letter o with diaeresis
U04EB	ӫ ӫ ӫ	`" ө`	Cyrillic small letter barred o with diaeresis
U04ED	ӭ ӭ ӭ	`" э`	Cyrillic small letter e with diaeresis
U04EF	ӯ ӯ ӯ	`_ y` `¯ y`	Cyrillic small letter u with macron
U04F1	ӱ ӱ ӱ	`" y`	Cyrillic small letter u with diaeresis
U04F3	ӳ ӳ ӳ	`= y`	Cyrillic small letter u with double acute

Unicode	Character	1 2 3 4	Name
U04F5	ӵ ӵ ӵ	" ч	Cyrillic small letter che with diaeresis
U04F9	ӹ ӹ ӹ	" ы	Cyrillic small letter yeru with diaeresis
U1E03	ḃ ḃ ḃ	. b b .	Latin small letter b with dot above
U1E05	ḅ ḅ ḅ	! b	Latin small letter b with dot below
U1E09	ḉ ḉ ḉ	' , c ' ç ´ , c ´ ç	Latin small letter c with cedilla and acute
U1E0B	ḋ ḋ ḋ	. d d .	Latin small letter d with dot above
U1E0D	ḍ ḍ ḍ	! d	Latin small letter d with dot below
U1E11	ḑ ḑ ḑ	, d d , , d	Latin small letter d with cedilla
U1E15	ḕ ḕ ḕ	` _ e ` ¯ e ` ē	Latin small letter e with macron and grave
U1E17	ḗ ḗ ḗ	' _ e ' ¯ e ' ē ´ _ e ´ ¯ e ´ ē	Latin small letter e with macron and acute
U1E1D	ḝ ḝ ḝ	U , e U ę U ␣ , e b , e b , e b ę	Latin small letter e with cedilla and breve
U1E1F	ḟ ḟ ḟ	. f f .	Latin small letter f with dot above
U1E21	ḡ ḡ ḡ	_ g ¯ g	Latin small letter g with macron
U1E23	ḣ ḣ ḣ	. h	Latin small letter h with dot above
U1E25	ḥ ḥ ḥ	! h	Latin small letter h with dot below
U1E27	ḧ ḧ ḧ	" h	Latin small letter h with diaeresis
U1E29	ḩ ḩ ḩ	, h h , , h	Latin small letter h with cedilla
U1E2F	ḯ ḯ ḯ	' " i ' ï ´ " i ´ ï	Latin small letter i with diaeresis and acute
U1E31	ḱ ḱ ḱ	' k ´ k	Latin small letter k with acute
U1E33	ḳ ḳ ḳ	! k	Latin small letter k with dot below
U1E37	ḷ ḷ ḷ	! l	Latin small letter l with dot below

Unicode	Character	1 2 3 4	Name
U1E39	ḹ ḷ ḻ	_!l	Latin small letter l with dot below and macron
		_ḷ	
		‾!l	
		‾ḷ	
U1E3F	ḿ ḿ ḿ	'm	Latin small letter m with acute
		´m	
U1E41	ṁ ṁ ṁ	.m	Latin small letter m with dot above
		m.	
U1E43	ṃ ṃ ṃ	!m	Latin small letter m with dot below
U1E45	ṅ ṅ ṅ	.n	Latin small letter n with dot above
U1E47	ṇ ṇ ṇ	!n	Latin small letter n with dot below
U1E4D	ṍ ṍ ṍ	'~o	Latin small letter o with tilde and acute
		'õ	
		´~o	
		´õ	
U1E4F	ṏ ṏ ṏ	"~o	Latin small letter o with tilde and diaeresis
		"õ	
U1E51	ṑ ṑ ṑ	`_o	Latin small letter o with macron and grave
		`‾o	
		`ō	
U1E53	ṓ ṓ ṓ	'_o	Latin small letter o with macron and acute
		'‾o	
		'ō	
		´_o	
		´‾o	
		´ō	
U1E55	ṕ ṕ ṕ	'p	Latin small letter p with acute
		´p	
U1E57	ṗ ṗ ṗ	.p	Latin small letter p with dot above
		p.	
U1E59	ṙ ṙ ṙ	.r	Latin small letter r with dot above
U1E5B	ṛ ṛ ṛ	!r	Latin small letter r with dot below
U1E5D	ṝ ṝ ṝ	_!r	Latin small letter r with dot below and macron
		_ṛ	
		‾!r	
		‾ṛ	
U1E61	ṡ ṡ ṡ	.s	Latin small letter s with dot above
		s.	
U1E63	ṣ ṣ ṣ	!s	Latin small letter s with dot below
U1E65	ṥ ṥ ṥ	.'s	Latin small letter s with acute and dot above
		.´s	
		.ś	
U1E67	ṧ ṧ ṧ	.š	Latin small letter s with caron and dot above
U1E69	ṩ ṩ ṩ	.!s	Latin small letter s with dot below and dot above
		.ṣ	
U1E6B	ṫ ṫ ṫ	.t	Latin small letter t with dot above
		t.	
U1E6D	ṭ ṭ ṭ	!t	Latin small letter t with dot below

Unicode	Character			1 2 3 4	Name
U1E79	ű	ű	ű	'~u	Latin small letter u with tilde and acute
				'~u	
				´~u	
				´ũ	
U1E7B	ṻ	ṻ	ṻ	"_u	Latin small letter u with macron and diaeresis
				"‾u	
				"ū	
U1E7D	ṽ	ṽ	ṽ	~v	Latin small letter v with tilde
U1E7F	ṿ	ṿ	ṿ	!v	Latin small letter v with dot below
U1E81	ẁ	ẁ	ẁ	`w	Latin small letter w with grave
U1E83	ẃ	ẃ	ẃ	'w	Latin small letter w with acute
				´w	
U1E85	ẅ	ẅ	ẅ	"w	Latin small letter w with diaeresis
U1E87	ẇ	ẇ	ẇ	.w	Latin small letter w with dot above
U1E89	ẉ	ẉ	ẉ	!w	Latin small letter w with dot below
U1E8B	ẋ	ẋ	ẋ	.x	Latin small letter x with dot above
U1E8D	ẍ	ẍ	ẍ	"x	Latin small letter x with diaeresis
U1E8F	ẏ	ẏ	ẏ	.y	Latin small letter y with dot above
U1E91	ẑ	ẑ	ẑ	^z	Latin small letter z with circumflex
U1E93	ẓ	ẓ	ẓ	!z	Latin small letter z with dot below
U1E97	ẗ	ẗ	ẗ	"t	Latin small letter t with diaeresis
U1E98	ẘ	ẘ	ẘ	ow	Latin small letter w with ring above
U1E99	ẙ	ẙ	ẙ	oy	Latin small letter y with ring above
U1E9B	ẛ	ẛ	ẛ	.ſ	Latin small letter long s with dot above
U1EA1	ạ	ạ	ạ	!a	Latin small letter a with dot below
U1EA3	ả	ả	ả	?a	Latin small letter a with hook above
U1EA5	ấ	ấ	ấ	'^a	Latin small letter a with circumflex and acute
				'â	
				´^a	
				´â	
U1EA7	ầ	ầ	ầ	`^a	Latin small letter a with circumflex and grave
				`â	
U1EA9	ẩ	ẩ	ẩ	?^a	Latin small letter a with circumflex and hook above
				?â	
U1EAB	ẫ	ẫ	ẫ	~^a	Latin small letter a with circumflex and tilde
				~â	
U1EAD	ậ	ậ	ậ	^!a	Latin small letter a with circumflex and dot below
				^ạ	
U1EAF	ắ	ắ	ắ	'ba	Latin small letter a with breve and acute
				'ă	
				´ba	
				´ă	
U1EB1	ằ	ằ	ằ	`ba	Latin small letter a with breve and grave
				`ă	
U1EB3	ẳ	ẳ	ẳ	?ba	Latin small letter a with breve and hook above
				?ă	
U1EB5	ẵ	ẵ	ẵ	~ba	Latin small letter a with breve and tilde
				~ă	

Unicode	Character	1 2 3 4	Name
U1EB7	ặ ặ ặ	U!a Uạ b!a bạ	Latin small letter a with breve and dot below
U1EB9	ẹ ẹ ẹ	!e	Latin small letter e with dot below
U1EBB	ẻ ẻ ẻ	?e	Latin small letter e with hook above
U1EBD	ẽ ẽ ẽ	~e	Latin small letter e with tilde
U1EBF	ế ế ế	'^e 'ê ´^e ´ê	Latin small letter e with circumflex and acute
U1EC1	ề ề ề	`^e `ê	Latin small letter e with circumflex and grave
U1EC3	ể ể ể	?^e ?ê	Latin small letter e with circumflex and hook above
U1EC5	ễ ễ ễ	~^e ~ê	Latin small letter e with circumflex and tilde
U1EC7	ệ ệ ệ	^!e ^ẹ	Latin small letter e with circumflex and dot below
U1EC9	ỉ ỉ ỉ	?i	Latin small letter i with hook above
U1ECB	ị ị ị	!i	Latin small letter i with dot below
U1ECD	ọ ọ ọ	!o	Latin small letter o with dot below
U1ECF	ỏ ỏ ỏ	?o	Latin small letter o with hook above
U1ED1	ố ố ố	'^o 'ô ´^o ´ô	Latin small letter o with circumflex and acute
U1ED3	ồ ồ ồ	`^o `ô	Latin small letter o with circumflex and grave
U1ED5	ổ ổ ổ	?^o ?ô	Latin small letter o with circumflex and hook above
U1ED7	ỗ ỗ ỗ	~^o ~ô	Latin small letter o with circumflex and tilde
U1ED9	ộ ộ ộ	^!o ^ọ	Latin small letter o with circumflex and dot below
U1EDB	ớ ớ ớ	'+o 'ơ ´+o ´ơ	Latin small letter o with horn and acute
U1EDD	ờ ờ ờ	`+o `ơ	Latin small letter o with horn and grave
U1EDF	ở ở ở	?+o ?ơ	Latin small letter o with horn and hook above
U1EE1	ỡ ỡ ỡ	~+o ~ơ	Latin small letter o with horn and tilde
U1EE3	ợ ợ ợ	!+o !ơ	Latin small letter o with horn and dot below
U1EE5	ụ ụ ụ	!u	Latin small letter u with dot below
U1EE7	ủ ủ ủ	?u	Latin small letter u with hook above

Unicode	Character	1234	Name

U1EE9	ứ ứ ứ	`'+u`
		`'ư`
		`´+u`
		`´ư`
			Latin small letter u with horn and acute

U1EEB	ừ ừ ừ	`` `+u `` `` `ư ``	Latin small letter u with horn and grave
U1EED	ử ử ử	`?+u` `?ư`	Latin small letter u with horn and hook above
U1EEF	ữ ữ ữ	`~+u` `~ư`	Latin small letter u with horn and tilde
U1EF1	ự ự ự	`!+u` `!ư`	Latin small letter u with horn and dot below
U1EF3	ỳ ỳ ỳ	`` `y ``	Latin small letter y with grave
U1EF5	ỵ ỵ ỵ	`!y`	Latin small letter y with dot below
U1EF7	ỷ ỷ ỷ	`?y`	Latin small letter y with hook above
U1EF9	ỹ ỹ ỹ	`~y`	Latin small letter y with tilde
U1F00	ἀ ἀ ἀ	`)α`	Greek small letter alpha with psili
U1F01	ἁ ἁ ἁ	`(α`	Greek small letter alpha with dasia
U1F02	ἂ ἂ ἂ	`` `)α `` `` `ά ``	Greek small letter alpha with psili and varia
U1F03	ἃ ἃ ἃ	`` `(α `` `` `ὰ ``	Greek small letter alpha with dasia and varia

U1F04	ἄ ἄ ἄ	`')α`
		`'ά`
		`´)α`
		`´ά`
			Greek small letter alpha with psili and oxia

U1F05	ἅ ἅ ἅ	`'(α`
		`'ὰ`
		`´(α`
		`´ὰ`
			Greek small letter alpha with dasia and oxia

U1F06	ἆ ἆ ἆ	`~)α` `~ά`	Greek small letter alpha with psili and perispomeni
U1F07	ἇ ἇ ἇ	`~(α` `~ὰ`	Greek small letter alpha with dasia and perispomeni
U1F10	ἐ ἐ ἐ	`)ε`	Greek small letter epsilon with psili
U1F11	ἑ ἑ ἑ	`(ε`	Greek small letter epsilon with dasia
U1F12	ἒ ἒ ἒ	`` `)ε `` `` `έ ``	Greek small letter epsilon with psili and varia
U1F13	ἓ ἓ ἓ	`` `(ε `` `` `ὲ ``	Greek small letter epsilon with dasia and varia

U1F14	ἔ ἔ ἔ	`')ε`
		`'έ`
		`´)ε`
		`´έ`
			Greek small letter epsilon with psili and oxia

U1F15	ἕ ἕ ἕ	`'(ε`
		`'ὲ`
		`´(ε`
		`´ὲ`
			Greek small letter epsilon with dasia and oxia

U1F20	ἠ ἠ ἠ	`)η`	Greek small letter eta with psili
U1F21	ἡ ἡ ἡ	`(η`	Greek small letter eta with dasia

Unicode	Character			1 2 3 4	Name
U1F22	ἢ	ἢ	ἢ	`)η `ή	Greek small letter eta with psili and varia
U1F23	ἣ	ἣ	ἣ	` (η `ή	Greek small letter eta with dasia and varia
U1F24	ἤ	ἤ	ἤ	')η 'ή ´)η ´ή	Greek small letter eta with psili and oxia
U1F25	ἥ	ἥ	ἥ	' (η 'ή ´ (η ´ή	Greek small letter eta with dasia and oxia
U1F26	ἦ	ἦ	ἦ	~)η ~ή	Greek small letter eta with psili and perispomeni
U1F27	ἧ	ἧ	ἧ	~ (η ~ή	Greek small letter eta with dasia and perispomeni
U1F30	ἰ	ἰ	ἰ	)ι	Greek small letter iota with psili
U1F31	ἱ	ἱ	ἱ	(ι	Greek small letter iota with dasia
U1F32	ἲ	ἲ	ἲ	`)ι `ι	Greek small letter iota with psili and varia
U1F33	ἳ	ἳ	ἳ	` (ι `ι	Greek small letter iota with dasia and varia
U1F34	ἴ	ἴ	ἴ	')ι 'ι ´)ι ´ι	Greek small letter iota with psili and oxia
U1F35	ἵ	ἵ	ἵ	' (ι 'ι ´ (ι ´ι	Greek small letter iota with dasia and oxia
U1F36	ἶ	ἶ	ἶ	~)ι ~ι	Greek small letter iota with psili and perispomeni
U1F37	ἷ	ἷ	ἷ	~ (ι ~ι	Greek small letter iota with dasia and perispomeni
U1F40	ὀ	ὀ	ὀ	)ο	Greek small letter omicron with psili
U1F41	ὁ	ὁ	ὁ	(ο	Greek small letter omicron with dasia
U1F42	ὂ	ὂ	ὂ	`)ο `ò	Greek small letter omicron with psili and varia
U1F43	ὃ	ὃ	ὃ	` (ο `ò	Greek small letter omicron with dasia and varia
U1F44	ὄ	ὄ	ὄ	')ο 'ò ´)ο ´ò	Greek small letter omicron with psili and oxia
U1F45	ὅ	ὅ	ὅ	' (ο 'ò ´ (ο ´ò	Greek small letter omicron with dasia and oxia
U1F50	ὐ	ὐ	ὐ	)υ	Greek small letter upsilon with psili
U1F51	ὑ	ὑ	ὑ	(υ	Greek small letter upsilon with dasia

Unicode	Character	1 2 3 4	Name
U1F52	ὒ ὒ ὒ	`) υ   `ύ	Greek small letter upsilon with psili and varia
U1F53	ὓ ὓ ὓ	` (υ   `ὺ	Greek small letter upsilon with dasia and varia
U1F54	ὔ ὔ ὔ	') υ ' ύ ´) υ ´ύ	Greek small letter upsilon with psili and oxia
U1F55	ὕ ὕ ὕ	' (υ ' ὺ ´ (υ ´ὺ	Greek small letter upsilon with dasia and oxia
U1F56	ὖ ὖ ὖ	~) υ ~ύ	Greek small letter upsilon with psili and perispomeni
U1F57	ὗ ὗ ὗ	~ (υ ~ὺ	Greek small letter upsilon with dasia and perispomeni
U1F60	ὠ ὠ ὠ	) ω	Greek small letter omega with psili
U1F61	ὡ ὡ ὡ	(ω	Greek small letter omega with dasia
U1F62	ὢ ὢ ὢ	` ) ω   `ώ	Greek small letter omega with psili and varia
U1F63	ὣ ὣ ὣ	` (ω   `ὼ	Greek small letter omega with dasia and varia
U1F64	ὤ ὤ ὤ	') ω ' ώ ´) ω ´ώ	Greek small letter omega with psili and oxia
U1F65	ὥ ὥ ὥ	' (ω ' ὼ ´ (ω ´ὼ	Greek small letter omega with dasia and oxia
U1F66	ὦ ὦ ὦ	~) ω ~ώ	Greek small letter omega with psili and perispomeni
U1F67	ὧ ὧ ὧ	~ (ω ~ὼ	Greek small letter omega with dasia and perispomeni
U1F70	ὰ ὰ ὰ	` α	Greek small letter alpha with varia
U1F72	ὲ ὲ ὲ	` ε	Greek small letter epsilon with varia
U1F74	ὴ ὴ ὴ	` η	Greek small letter eta with varia
U1F76	ὶ ὶ ὶ	` ι	Greek small letter iota with varia
U1F78	ὸ ὸ ὸ	` ο	Greek small letter omicron with varia
U1F7A	ὺ ὺ ὺ	` υ	Greek small letter upsilon with varia
U1F7C	ὼ ὼ ὼ	` ω	Greek small letter omega with varia
U1F80	ᾀ ᾀ ᾀ	ι) α ιά	Greek small letter alpha with psili and ypogegrammeni
U1F81	ᾁ ᾁ ᾁ	ι (α ιά	Greek small letter alpha with dasia and ypogegrammeni
U1F82	ᾂ ᾂ ᾂ	ι ` ) α   ι ` ά ιὰ	Greek small letter alpha with psili and varia and ypogegrammeni
U1F83	ᾃ ᾃ ᾃ	ι ` (α   ι ` ά ιὰ	Greek small letter alpha with dasia and varia and ypogegrammeni

Unicode	Character	1 2 3 4	Name
U1F84	ᾄ ᾄ ᾄ	ι ') α ι ' ά ι ´) α ι ´ ά ιᾄ	Greek small letter alpha with psili and oxia and ypogegrammeni
U1F85	ᾅ ᾅ ᾅ	ι ' (α ι ' ὰ ι ´ (α ι ´ ὰ ιᾅ	Greek small letter alpha with dasia and oxia and ypogegrammeni
U1F86	ᾆ ᾆ ᾆ	ι ~) α ι ~ ά ιᾆ	Greek small letter alpha with psili and perispomeni and ypogegrammeni
U1F87	ᾇ ᾇ ᾇ	ι ~ (α ι ~ ὰ ιᾇ	Greek small letter alpha with dasia and perispomeni and ypogegrammeni
U1F90	ᾐ ᾐ ᾐ	ι) η ιή	Greek small letter eta with psili and ypogegrammeni
U1F91	ᾑ ᾑ ᾑ	ι (η ιή	Greek small letter eta with dasia and ypogegrammeni
U1F92	ᾒ ᾒ ᾒ	ι ` ) η ι ` ή ιῆ	Greek small letter eta with psili and varia and ypogegrammeni
U1F93	ᾓ ᾓ ᾓ	ι ` ( η ι ` ή ιῆ	Greek small letter eta with dasia and varia and ypogegrammeni
U1F94	ᾔ ᾔ ᾔ	ι ') η ι ' ή ι ´) η ι ´ ή ιή	Greek small letter eta with psili and oxia and ypogegrammeni
U1F95	ᾕ ᾕ ᾕ	ι ' (η ι ' ή ι ´ (η ι ´ ή ιή	Greek small letter eta with dasia and oxia and ypogegrammeni
U1F96	ᾖ ᾖ ᾖ	ι ~) η ι ~ ή ιῆ	Greek small letter eta with psili and perispomeni and ypogegrammeni
U1F97	ᾗ ᾗ ᾗ	ι ~ (η ι ~ ή ιῆ	Greek small letter eta with dasia and perispomeni and ypogegrammeni
U1FA0	ᾠ ᾠ ᾠ	ι) ω ιώ	Greek small letter omega with psili and ypogegrammeni
U1FA1	ᾡ ᾡ ᾡ	ι (ω ιώ	Greek small letter omega with dasia and ypogegrammeni
U1FA2	ᾢ ᾢ ᾢ	ι ` ) ω ι ` ώ ιῶ	Greek small letter omega with psili and varia and ypogegrammeni

Unicode	Character	1 2 3 4	Name
U1FA3	ῷ ῷ ῷ	ι ` (ω ι ` ὼ ιὼ	Greek small letter omega with dasia and varia and ypogegrammeni
U1FA4	ῴ ῴ ῴ	ι ') ω ι ' ώ ι ´) ω ι ´ ώ ιώ	Greek small letter omega with psili and oxia and ypogegrammeni
U1FA5	ῴ ῴ ῴ	ι ' (ω ι ' ὼ ι ´ (ω ι ´ ὼ ιώ	Greek small letter omega with dasia and oxia and ypogegrammeni
U1FA6	ῶ ῶ ῶ	ι ~) ω ι ~ ῶ ιῶ	Greek small letter omega with psili and perispomeni and ypogegrammeni
U1FA7	ῷ ῷ ῷ	ι ~ (ω ι ~ ὼ ιῶ	Greek small letter omega with dasia and perispomeni and ypogegrammeni
U1FB0	ᾰ ᾰ ᾰ	Uα bα	Greek small letter alpha with vrachy
U1FB1	ᾱ ᾱ ᾱ	_α ¯α	Greek small letter alpha with macron
U1FB2	ᾲ ᾲ ᾲ	ι ` α ιὰ	Greek small letter alpha with varia and ypogegrammeni
U1FB3	ᾳ ᾳ ᾳ	ια	Greek small letter alpha with ypogegrammeni
U1FB4	ᾴ ᾴ ᾴ	ι ' α ι ´ α ιά	Greek small letter alpha with oxia and ypogegrammeni
U1FB6	ᾶ ᾶ ᾶ	~α	Greek small letter alpha with perispomeni
U1FB7	ᾷ ᾷ ᾷ	ι ~ α ιᾶ	Greek small letter alpha with perispomeni and ypogegrammeni
U1FC2	ῂ ῂ ῂ	ι ` η ιὴ	Greek small letter eta with varia and ypogegrammeni
U1FC3	ῃ ῃ ῃ	ιη	Greek small letter eta with ypogegrammeni
U1FC4	ῄ ῄ ῄ	ι ' η ι ´ η ιή	Greek small letter eta with oxia and ypogegrammeni
U1FC6	ῆ ῆ ῆ	~η	Greek small letter eta with perispomeni
U1FC7	ῇ ῇ ῇ	ι ~ η ιῆ	Greek small letter eta with perispomeni and ypogegrammeni
U1FD0	ῐ ῐ ῐ	Uι bι	Greek small letter iota with vrachy
U1FD1	ῑ ῑ ῑ	_ι ¯ι	Greek small letter iota with macron
U1FD2	ῒ ῒ ῒ	` " ι ` ϊ	Greek small letter iota with dialytika and varia
U1FD6	ῖ ῖ ῖ	~ι	Greek small letter iota with perispomeni
U1FD7	ῗ ῗ ῗ	~ " ι ~ ϊ	Greek small letter iota with dialytika and perispomeni

Unicode	Character			1 2 3 4	Name
U1FE0	Ῠ	ῠ	ῠ	Uʊ bʊ	Greek small letter upsilon with vrachy
U1FE1	Ῡ	ῡ	ῡ	_ʊ ¯ʊ	Greek small letter upsilon with macron
U1FE2	Ϋ̀	ῢ	ῢ	` "ʊ ` ϋ	Greek small letter upsilon with dialytika and varia
U1FE4	ῤ	ῤ	ῤ	) ρ	Greek small letter rho with psili
U1FE5	ῥ	ῥ	ῥ	(ρ	Greek small letter rho with dasia
U1FE6	Υ͂	ῦ	ῦ	~ʊ	Greek small letter upsilon with perispomeni
U1FE7	Ϋ͂	ῧ	ῧ	~ "ʊ ~ ϋ	Greek small letter upsilon with dialytika and perispomeni
U1FF2	ῲ	ῲ	ῲ	ι`ω ιὼ	Greek small letter omega with varia and ypogegrammeni
U1FF3	ῳ	ῳ	ῳ	ιω	Greek small letter omega with ypogegrammeni
U1FF4	ῴ	ῴ	ῴ	ι'ω ι´ω ιό	Greek small letter omega with oxia and ypogegrammeni
U1FF6	ῶ	ῶ	ῶ	~ω	Greek small letter omega with perispomeni
U1FF7	ῷ	ῷ	ῷ	ι~ω ιῶ	Greek small letter omega with perispomeni and ypogegrammeni
UFB00	ﬀ	ﬀ	ﬀ	ff	Latin small ligature ff
UFB01	ﬁ	ﬁ	ﬁ	fi	Latin small ligature fi
UFB02	ﬂ	ﬂ	ﬂ	fl	Latin small ligature fl
UFB03	ﬃ	ﬃ	ﬃ	Fi	Latin small ligature ffi
UFB04	ﬄ	ﬄ	ﬄ	Fl	Latin small ligature ffl

2.2 Letter, Uppercase (Lu)

Unicode	Character			1 2 3 4	Name
U00C0	À	À	À	A` ` A	Latin capital letter a with grave
U00C1	Á	Á	Á	'A A' A´ ´A	Latin capital letter a with acute
U00C2	Â	Â	Â	>A A> A^ ^A	Latin capital letter a with circumflex
U00C3	Ã	Ã	Ã	A~ ~A	Latin capital letter a with tilde
U00C4	Ä	Ä	Ä	"A A" A¨ ¨A	Latin capital letter a with diaeresis
U00C5	Å	Å	Å	*A A* AA oA	Latin capital letter a with ring above
U00C6	Æ	Æ	Æ	AE	Latin capital letter ae

Unicode	Character	1 2 3 4	Name
U00C7	Ç Ç ç	, C C , ¸ C	Latin capital letter c with cedilla
U00C8	È È è	E ` ` E	Latin capital letter e with grave
U00C9	É É é	' E E ' E ´ ´ E	Latin capital letter e with acute
U00CA	Ê Ê ê	> E E > E ^ ^ E	Latin capital letter e with circumflex
U00CB	Ë Ë ë	" E E " E ¨ ¨ E	Latin capital letter e with diaeresis
U00CC	Ì Ì ì	I ` ` I	Latin capital letter i with grave
U00CD	Í Í í	' I I ' I ´ ´ I	Latin capital letter i with acute
U00CE	Î Î î	> I I > I ^ ^ I	Latin capital letter i with circumflex
U00CF	Ï Ï ï	" I I " I ¨ ¨ I	Latin capital letter i with diaeresis
U00D0	Ð Ð ð	DH	Latin capital letter eth
U00D1	Ñ Ñ ñ	N ~ ~ N	Latin capital letter n with tilde
U00D2	Ò Ò ò	O ` ` O	Latin capital letter o with grave
U00D3	Ó Ó ó	' O O ' U ˙ ´ O	Latin capital letter o with acute
U00D4	Ô Ô ô	> O O > O ^ ^ O	Latin capital letter o with circumflex
U00D5	Õ Õ õ	O ~ ~ O	Latin capital letter o with tilde
U00D6	Ö Ö ö	" O O " O ¨ ¨ O	Latin capital letter o with diaeresis

Unicode	Character	1 2 3 4	Name
U00D8	Ø Ø ø	/O O/	Latin capital letter o with stroke
U00D9	Ù Ù ù	U\` \`U	Latin capital letter u with grave
U00DA	Ú Ú ú	'U U' U´ ´U	Latin capital letter u with acute
U00DB	Û Û û	>U U> U^ ^U	Latin capital letter u with circumflex
U00DC	Ü Ü ü	"U U" U¨ ¨U	Latin capital letter u with diaeresis
U00DD	Ý Ý ý	'Y Y' Y´ ´Y	Latin capital letter y with acute
U00DE	Þ Þ þ	TH	Latin capital letter thorn
U0100	Ā Ā ā	-A -a A- A_ _A a- ¯A	Latin capital letter a with macron
U0102	Ă Ă ă	A(UA bA	Latin capital letter a with breve
U0104	Ą Ą ą	,A ;A A,	Latin capital letter a with ogonek
U0106	Ć Ć ć	'C C' ´C	Latin capital letter c with acute
U0108	Ĉ Ĉ ĉ	^C	Latin capital letter c with circumflex
U010A	Ċ Ċ ċ	.C C.	Latin capital letter c with dot above
U010C	Č Č č	<C C< cC	Latin capital letter c with caron
U010E	Ď Ď ď	<D D< cD	Latin capital letter d with caron
U0110	Đ Đ đ	-D /D D-	Latin capital letter d with stroke

Unicode	Character	1 2 3 4	Name
U0112	Ē Ē ē	−E E− E_ _E ¯E	Latin capital letter e with macron
U0114	Ĕ Ĕ ĕ	UE bE	Latin capital letter e with breve
U0116	Ė Ė ė	.E E.	Latin capital letter e with dot above
U0118	Ę Ę ę	,E ;E E,	Latin capital letter e with ogonek
U011A	Ě Ě ě	<E E< cE	Latin capital letter e with caron
U011C	Ĝ Ĝ ĝ	^G	Latin capital letter g with circumflex
U011E	Ğ Ğ ğ	G(GU G˘ UG bG ˘G	Latin capital letter g with breve
U0120	Ġ Ġ ġ	.G G.	Latin capital letter g with dot above
U0122	Ģ Ģ ģ	,G G, ¸G	Latin capital letter g with cedilla
U0124	Ĥ Ĥ ĥ	^H	Latin capital letter h with circumflex
U0126	Ħ Ħ ħ	/H	Latin capital letter h with stroke
U0128	Ĩ Ĩ ĩ	I~ ~I	Latin capital letter i with tilde
U012A	Ī Ī ī	−I I− I_ _I ¯I	Latin capital letter i with macron
U012C	Ĭ Ĭ ĭ	UI bI	Latin capital letter i with breve
U012E	Į Į į	,I ;I I,	Latin capital letter i with ogonek
U0130	İ İ i̇	.I I.	Latin capital letter i with dot above
U0132	Ĳ Ĳ ĳ	IJ Ij	Latin capital ligature ij
U0134	Ĵ Ĵ ĵ	^J	Latin capital letter j with circumflex
U0136	Ķ Ķ ķ	,K K, ¸K	Latin capital letter k with cedilla

Unicode	Character	1 2 3 4	Name
U0139	Ĺ Ĺ ĺ	'L L' ´L	Latin capital letter l with acute
U013B	Ļ Ļ ļ	,L L, ،L	Latin capital letter l with cedilla
U013D	Ľ Ľ ľ	<L L< cL	Latin capital letter l with caron
U0141	Ł Ł ł	/L L/	Latin capital letter l with stroke
U0143	Ń Ń ń	'N N' ´N	Latin capital letter n with acute
U0145	Ņ Ņ ņ	,N N, ،N	Latin capital letter n with cedilla
U0147	Ň Ň ň	<N N< cN	Latin capital letter n with caron
U014A	Ŋ Ŋ ŋ	NG	Latin capital letter eng
U014C	Ō Ō ō	-O O- O_ _O ¯O	Latin capital letter o with macron
U014E	Ŏ Ŏ ŏ	UO bO	Latin capital letter o with breve
U0150	Ő Ő ő	=O	Latin capital letter o with double acute
U0152	Œ Œ œ	OE	Latin capital ligature oe
U0154	Ŕ Ŕ ŕ	'R R' ´R	Latin capital letter r with acute
U0156	Ŗ Ŗ ŗ	,R R, ،R	Latin capital letter r with cedilla
U0158	Ř Ř ř	<R R< cR	Latin capital letter r with caron
U015A	Ś Ś ś	'S S' ´S	Latin capital letter s with acute
U015C	Ŝ Ŝ ŝ	^S	Latin capital letter s with circumflex
U015E	Ş Ş ş	,S S, ،S	Latin capital letter s with cedilla
U0160	Š Š š	<S S< cS	Latin capital letter s with caron

Unicode	Character	1234	Name
U0162	Ţ Ţ ţ	, T T , . T	Latin capital letter t with cedilla
U0164	Ť Ť ť	<T T< cT	Latin capital letter t with caron
U0166	Ŧ Ŧ ŧ	/T T- T/	Latin capital letter t with stroke
U0168	Ũ Ũ ũ	U~ ~U	Latin capital letter u with tilde
U016A	Ū Ū ū	-U U- U_ _U ‾U	Latin capital letter u with macron
U016C	Ŭ Ŭ ŭ	UU bU	Latin capital letter u with breve
U016E	Ů Ů ů	*U U* oU	Latin capital letter u with ring above
U0170	Ű Ű ű	=U	Latin capital letter u with double acute
U0172	Ų Ų ų	, U ; U U ,	Latin capital letter u with ogonek
U0174	Ŵ Ŵ ŵ	W^ ^W	Latin capital letter w with circumflex
U0176	Ŷ Ŷ ŷ	Y^ ^Y	Latin capital letter y with circumflex
U0178	Ÿ Ÿ ÿ	"Y Y" Y¨ ¨Y	Latin capital letter y with diaeresis
U0179	Ź Ź ź	'Z Z' ´Z	Latin capital letter z with acute
U017B	Ż Ż ż	.Z Z.	Latin capital letter z with dot above
U017D	Ž Ž ž	<Z Z< cZ vZ	Latin capital letter z with caron
U0197	Ɨ Ɨ ɨ	/I	Latin capital letter i with stroke
U01A0	Ơ Ơ ơ	+O	Latin capital letter o with horn
U01AF	Ư Ư ư	+U	Latin capital letter u with horn
U01B5	Ƶ Ƶ ƶ	/Z	Latin capital letter z with stroke
U01CD	Ǎ Ǎ ǎ	cA	Latin capital letter a with caron
U01CF	Ǐ Ǐ ǐ	cI	Latin capital letter i with caron
U01D1	Ǒ Ǒ ǒ	cO	Latin capital letter o with caron
U01D3	Ǔ Ǔ ǔ	cU	Latin capital letter u with caron

Unicode	Character	1 2 3 4	Name
U01D5	Ǖ Ǖ ǖ	_"U _Ü ⁻"U ⁻Ü	Latin capital letter u with diaeresis and macron
U01D7	Ǘ Ǘ ǘ	'"U 'Ü ´"U ´Ü	Latin capital letter u with diaeresis and acute
U01D9	Ǚ Ǚ ǚ	c"U cÜ	Latin capital letter u with diaeresis and caron
U01DB	Ǜ Ǜ ǜ	`"U `Ü	Latin capital letter u with diaeresis and grave
U01DE	Ǟ Ǟ ǟ	_"A _Ä ⁻"A ⁻Ä	Latin capital letter a with diaeresis and macron
U01E0	Ǡ Ǡ ǡ	_.A _Ȧ ⁻.A ⁻Ȧ	Latin capital letter a with dot above and macron
U01E2	Ǣ Ǣ ǣ	_Æ ⁻Æ	Latin capital letter ae with macron
U01E4	Ǥ Ǥ ǥ	/G	Latin capital letter g with stroke
U01E6	Ǧ Ǧ ǧ	cG	Latin capital letter g with caron
U01E8	Ǩ Ǩ ǩ	cK	Latin capital letter k with caron
U01EA	Ǫ Ǫ ǫ	;O	Latin capital letter o with ogonek
U01EC	Ǭ Ǭ ǭ	_;O _Ǫ ⁻;O ⁻Ǫ	Latin capital letter o with ogonek and macron
U01EE	Ǯ Ǯ ǯ	c3	Latin capital letter ezh with caron
U01F4	Ǵ Ǵ ǵ	'G ´G	Latin capital letter g with acute
U01F8	Ǹ Ǹ ǹ	`N	Latin capital letter n with grave
U01FA	Ǻ Ǻ ǻ	'Å *'A ´Å	Latin capital letter a with ring above and acute
U01FC	Ǽ Ǽ ǽ	'Æ ´Æ	Latin capital letter ae with acute
U01FE	Ǿ Ǿ ǿ	'/O 'Ø ´/O ´Ø	Latin capital letter o with stroke and acute
U021E	Ȟ Ȟ ȟ	cH	Latin capital letter h with caron
U0226	Ȧ Ȧ ȧ	.A	Latin capital letter a with dot above
U0228	Ȩ Ȩ ȩ	,E	Latin capital letter e with cedilla
U022A	Ȫ Ȫ ȫ	_"O _Ö ⁻"O ⁻Ö	Latin capital letter o with diaeresis and macron

Unicode	Character	1 2 3 4	Name
U022C	Ȭ Ȭ ȭ	_~O _Õ ¯~O ¯Õ	Latin capital letter o with tilde and macron
U022E	Ȯ Ȯ ȯ	.O	Latin capital letter o with dot above
U0230	Ȱ Ȱ ȱ	_.O _Ȯ ¯.O ¯Ȯ	Latin capital letter o with dot above and macron
U0232	Ȳ Ȳ ȳ	_Y ¯Y	Latin capital letter y with macron
U0386	Ά Ά ΐ	'A ´A A'	Greek capital letter alpha with tonos
U0388	Έ Έ ΐ	'E ´E E'	Greek capital letter epsilon with tonos
U0389	Ή Ή ΐ	'H ´H H'	Greek capital letter eta with tonos
U038A	Ί Ί ΐ	'I ´I I'	Greek capital letter iota with tonos
U038C	Ό Ό ΐ	'O ´O O'	Greek capital letter omicron with tonos
U038E	Ύ Ύ ΐ	'Y ´Y Y'	Greek capital letter upsilon with tonos
U038F	Ώ Ώ ΐ	'Ω ´Ω Ω'	Greek capital letter omega with tonos
U03AA	Ϊ Ϊ ΐ	"I I"	Greek capital letter iota with dialytika
U03AB	Ϋ Ϋ ΐ	"Y Y"	Greek capital letter upsilon with dialytika
U03D4	Ϋ Ϋ ΐ	"Y	Greek upsilon with diaeresis and hook symbol
U0400	Ѐ Ѐ ѐ	`E	Cyrillic capital letter ie with grave
U0401	Ё Ё ё	"E	Cyrillic capital letter io
U0403	Ѓ Ѓ ѓ	'Г ´Г	Cyrillic capital letter gje
U0407	Ї Ї ї	"I	Cyrillic capital letter yi
U040C	Ќ Ќ ќ	'K ´K	Cyrillic capital letter kje
U040D	Ѝ Ѝ ѝ	`И	Cyrillic capital letter i with grave
U040E	Ў Ў ў	UY bY	Cyrillic capital letter short u
U0419	Й Й й	UИ bИ	Cyrillic capital letter short i
U0492	Ғ Ғ ғ	/Г	Cyrillic capital letter ghe with stroke
U049E	Ҟ Ҟ ҟ	/K	Cyrillic capital letter ka with stroke

Unicode	Character	1 2 3 4	Name
U04B0	Ұ Ұ ұ	/Y	Cyrillic capital letter straight u with stroke
U04C1	Ӂ Ӂ ӂ	UЖ bЖ	Cyrillic capital letter zhe with breve
U04D0	Ӑ Ӑ ӑ	UA bA	Cyrillic capital letter a with breve
U04D2	Ӓ Ӓ ӓ	"A	Cyrillic capital letter a with diaeresis
U04D6	Ӗ Ӗ ӗ	UE bE	Cyrillic capital letter ie with breve
U04DA	Ӛ Ӛ ӛ	"ə	Cyrillic capital letter schwa with diaeresis
U04DC	Ӝ Ӝ ӝ	"Ж	Cyrillic capital letter zhe with diaeresis
U04DE	Ӟ Ӟ ӟ	"З	Cyrillic capital letter ze with diaeresis
U04E2	Ӣ Ӣ ӣ	_И ‾И	Cyrillic capital letter i with macron
U04E4	Ӥ Ӥ ӥ	"И	Cyrillic capital letter i with diaeresis
U04E6	Ӧ Ӧ ӧ	"О	Cyrillic capital letter o with diaeresis
U04EA	Ӫ Ӫ ӫ	"Ө	Cyrillic capital letter barred o with diaeresis
U04EC	Ӭ Ӭ ӭ	"Э	Cyrillic capital letter e with diaeresis
U04EE	Ӯ Ӯ ӯ	_У ‾У	Cyrillic capital letter u with macron
U04F0	Ӱ Ӱ ӱ	"У	Cyrillic capital letter u with diaeresis
U04F2	Ӳ Ӳ ӳ	=У	Cyrillic capital letter u with double acute
U04F4	Ӵ Ӵ ӵ	"Ч	Cyrillic capital letter che with diaeresis
U04F8	Ӹ Ӹ ӹ	"Ы	Cyrillic capital letter yeru with diaeresis
U1E02	Ḃ Ḃ ḃ	.B B.	Latin capital letter b with dot above
U1E04	Ḅ Ḅ ḅ	!B	Latin capital letter b with dot below
U1E08	Ḉ Ḉ ḉ	' ˛C 'Ç ´ ˛C ´ ˛C ´Ç	Latin capital letter c with cedilla and acute
U1E0A	Ḋ Ḋ ḋ	.D D.	Latin capital letter d with dot above
U1E0C	Ḍ Ḍ ḍ	!D	Latin capital letter d with dot below
U1E10	Ḑ Ḑ ḑ	,D D, ˛D	Latin capital letter d with cedilla
U1E14	Ḕ Ḕ ḕ	`_E ` ‾E `Ē	Latin capital letter e with macron and grave
U1E16	Ḗ Ḗ ḗ	'_E ' ‾E 'Ē ´_E ´ ‾E ´Ē	Latin capital letter e with macron and acute

Unicode	Character	1234	Name
U1E1C	Ĕ Ĕ ĕ	U ̧ E U Ĕ U ̇ , E b , E b ̧ E b Ĕ	Latin capital letter e with cedilla and breve
U1E1E	Ḟ Ḟ ḟ	. F F .	Latin capital letter f with dot above
U1E20	Ḡ Ḡ ḡ	_ G ¯ G	Latin capital letter g with macron
U1E22	Ḣ Ḣ ḣ	. H	Latin capital letter h with dot above
U1E24	Ḥ Ḥ ḥ	! H	Latin capital letter h with dot below
U1E26	Ḧ Ḧ ḧ	" H	Latin capital letter h with diaeresis
U1E28	Ḩ Ḩ ḩ	, H H , ̧ H	Latin capital letter h with cedilla
U1E2E	Í̈ Í̈ í̈	' " I ' Ï ´ " I ´ Ï	Latin capital letter i with diaeresis and acute
U1E30	Ḱ Ḱ ḱ	' K ´ K	Latin capital letter k with acute
U1E32	Ḳ Ḳ ḳ	! K	Latin capital letter k with dot below
U1E36	Ḷ Ḷ ḷ	! L	Latin capital letter l with dot below
U1E38	Ḹ Ḹ ḹ	_ ! L _ Ḷ ¯ ! L ¯ Ḷ	Latin capital letter l with dot below and macron
U1E3E	Ḿ Ḿ ḿ	' M ´ M	Latin capital letter m with acute
U1E40	Ṁ Ṁ ṁ	. M M .	Latin capital letter m with dot above
U1E42	Ṃ Ṃ ṃ	! M	Latin capital letter m with dot below
U1E44	Ṅ Ṅ ṅ	. N	Latin capital letter n with dot above
U1E46	Ṇ Ṇ ṇ	! N	Latin capital letter n with dot below
U1E4C	Ṍ Ṍ ṍ	' ~ O ' Õ ´ ~ O ´ Õ	Latin capital letter o with tilde and acute
U1E4E	Ṏ Ṏ ṏ	" ~ O " Õ	Latin capital letter o with tilde and diaeresis
U1E50	Ṑ Ṑ ṑ	` _ O ` ¯ O ` Ō	Latin capital letter o with macron and grave
U1E52	Ṓ Ṓ ṓ	' _ O ' ¯ O ' Ō ´ _ O ´ ¯ O ´ Ō	Latin capital letter o with macron and acute

Unicode	Character	1 2 3 4	Name
U1E54	Ṕ Ṕ ṕ	' P ´ P	Latin capital letter p with acute
U1E56	Ṗ Ṗ ṗ	. P P .	Latin capital letter p with dot above
U1E58	Ṙ Ṙ ṙ	. R	Latin capital letter r with dot above
U1E5A	Ṛ Ṛ ṛ	! R	Latin capital letter r with dot below
U1E5C	Ṝ Ṝ ṝ	_ ! R _ Ṛ ‾ ! R ‾ Ṛ	Latin capital letter r with dot below and macron
U1E60	Ṡ Ṡ ṡ	. S S .	Latin capital letter s with dot above
U1E62	Ṣ Ṣ ṣ	! S	Latin capital letter s with dot below
U1E64	Ś Ś ś	. ' S . ´ S . ś	Latin capital letter s with acute and dot above
U1E66	Š Š š	. š	Latin capital letter s with caron and dot above
U1E68	Ṩ Ṩ ṩ	. ! S . Ṣ	Latin capital letter s with dot below and dot above
U1E6A	Ṫ Ṫ ṫ	. T T .	Latin capital letter t with dot above
U1E6C	Ṭ Ṭ ṭ	! T	Latin capital letter t with dot below
U1E78	Ṹ Ṹ ṹ	' ~ U ' Ũ ´ ~ U ´ Ũ	Latin capital letter u with tilde and acute
U1E7A	Ṻ Ṻ ṻ	" _ U " ‾ U " Ū	Latin capital letter u with macron and diaeresis
U1E7C	Ṽ Ṽ ṽ	~ V	Latin capital letter v with tilde
U1E7E	Ṿ Ṿ ṿ	! V	Latin capital letter v with dot below
U1E80	Ẁ Ẁ ẁ	` W	Latin capital letter w with grave
U1E82	Ẃ Ẃ ẃ	' W ´ W	Latin capital letter w with acute
U1E84	Ẅ Ẅ ẅ	" W	Latin capital letter w with diaeresis
U1E86	Ẇ Ẇ ẇ	. W	Latin capital letter w with dot above
U1E88	Ẉ Ẉ ẉ	! W	Latin capital letter w with dot below
U1E8A	Ẋ Ẋ ẋ	. X	Latin capital letter x with dot above
U1E8C	Ẍ Ẍ ẍ	" X	Latin capital letter x with diaeresis
U1E8E	Ẏ Ẏ ẏ	. Y	Latin capital letter y with dot above
U1E90	Ẑ Ẑ ẑ	^ Z	Latin capital letter z with circumflex
U1E92	Ẓ Ẓ ẓ	! Z	Latin capital letter z with dot below
U1E9E	ẞ ß	S S	Latin capital letter sharp s
U1EA0	Ạ Ạ ạ	! A	Latin capital letter a with dot below
U1EA2	Ả Ả ả	? A	Latin capital letter a with hook above
U1EA4	Ấ Ấ ấ	' ^ A ' Â ´ ^ A ´ Â	Latin capital letter a with circumflex and acute

Unicode	Character	1 2 3 4	Name
U1EA6	À Ầ Ầ	`` `^A `` `` `Â ``	Latin capital letter a with circumflex and grave
U1EA8	Ẩ Ẩ Ẩ	?^A ?Â	Latin capital letter a with circumflex and hook above
U1EAA	Ẫ Ẫ Ẫ	~^A ~Â	Latin capital letter a with circumflex and tilde
U1EAC	Ậ Ậ Ậ	^!A ^Ạ	Latin capital letter a with circumflex and dot below
U1EAE	Ắ Ắ Ắ	'bA 'Ă ´bA ´Ă	Latin capital letter a with breve and acute
U1EB0	Ằ Ằ Ằ	`` `bA `` `` `Ă ``	Latin capital letter a with breve and grave
U1EB2	Ẳ Ẳ Ẳ	?bA ?Ă	Latin capital letter a with breve and hook above
U1EB4	Ẵ Ẵ Ẵ	~bA ~Ă	Latin capital letter a with breve and tilde
U1EB6	Ặ Ặ Ặ	U!A UẠ b!A bẠ	Latin capital letter a with breve and dot below
U1EB8	Ẹ Ẹ Ẹ	!E	Latin capital letter e with dot below
U1EBA	Ẻ Ẻ Ẻ	?E	Latin capital letter e with hook above
U1EBC	Ẽ Ẽ Ẽ	~E	Latin capital letter e with tilde
U1EBE	Ế Ế Ế	'^E 'Ê ´^E ´Ê	Latin capital letter e with circumflex and acute
U1EC0	Ề Ề Ề	`` `^E `` `` `Ê ``	Latin capital letter e with circumflex and grave
U1EC2	Ể Ể Ể	?^E ?Ê	Latin capital letter e with circumflex and hook above
U1EC4	Ễ Ễ Ễ	~^E ~Ê	Latin capital letter e with circumflex and tilde
U1EC6	Ệ Ệ Ệ	^!E ^Ẹ	Latin capital letter e with circumflex and dot below
U1EC8	Ỉ Ỉ Ỉ	?I	Latin capital letter i with hook above
U1ECA	Ị Ị Ị	!I	Latin capital letter i with dot below
U1ECC	Ọ Ọ Ọ	!O	Latin capital letter o with dot below
U1ECE	Ỏ Ỏ Ỏ	?O	Latin capital letter o with hook above
U1ED0	Ố Ố Ố	'^O 'Ô ´^O ´Ô	Latin capital letter o with circumflex and acute
U1ED2	Ồ Ồ Ồ	`` `^O `` `` `Ô ``	Latin capital letter o with circumflex and grave
U1ED4	Ổ Ổ Ổ	?^O ?Ô	Latin capital letter o with circumflex and hook above

Unicode	Character	1 2 3 4	Name
U1ED6	Ỗ Ỗ ỗ	~^O ~ô	Latin capital letter o with circumflex and tilde
U1ED8	Ộ Ộ ộ	^!O ^ọ	Latin capital letter o with circumflex and dot below
U1EDA	Ớ Ớ ớ	'+O 'ơ ´+O ´ơ	Latin capital letter o with horn and acute
U1EDC	Ờ Ờ ờ	`+O `ơ	Latin capital letter o with horn and grave
U1EDE	Ở Ở ở	?+O ?ơ	Latin capital letter o with horn and hook above
U1EE0	Ỡ Ỡ ỡ	~+O ~ơ	Latin capital letter o with horn and tilde
U1EE2	Ợ Ợ ợ	!+O !ơ	Latin capital letter o with horn and dot below
U1EE4	Ụ Ụ ụ	!U	Latin capital letter u with dot below
U1EE6	Ủ Ủ ủ	?U	Latin capital letter u with hook above
U1EE8	Ứ Ứ ứ	'+U 'ư ´+U ´ư	Latin capital letter u with horn and acute
U1EEA	Ừ Ừ ừ	`+U `ư	Latin capital letter u with horn and grave
U1EEC	Ử Ử ử	?+U ?ư	Latin capital letter u with horn and hook above
U1EEE	Ữ Ữ ữ	~+U ~ư	Latin capital letter u with horn and tilde
U1EF0	Ự Ự ự	!+U !ư	Latin capital letter u with horn and dot below
U1EF2	Ỳ Ỳ ỳ	`Y	Latin capital letter y with grave
U1EF4	Ỵ Ỵ ỵ	!Y	Latin capital letter y with dot below
U1EF6	Ỷ Ỷ ỷ	?Y	Latin capital letter y with hook above
U1EF8	Ỹ Ỹ ỹ	~Y	Latin capital letter y with tilde
U1F08	Ἀ Ἀ Ἀ	)A	Greek capital letter alpha with psili
U1F09	Ἁ Ἁ Ἁ	(A	Greek capital letter alpha with dasia
U1F0A	Ἂ Ἂ Ἂ	`)A `Ἀ	Greek capital letter alpha with psili and varia
U1F0B	Ἃ Ἃ Ἃ	`(A `Ἁ	Greek capital letter alpha with dasia and varia
U1F0C	Ἄ Ἄ Ἄ	')A 'Ἀ ´)A ´Ἀ	Greek capital letter alpha with psili and oxia
U1F0D	Ἅ Ἅ Ἅ	'(A 'Ἁ ´(A ´Ἁ	Greek capital letter alpha with dasia and oxia
U1F0E	Ἆ Ἆ Ἆ	~)A ~Ἀ	Greek capital letter alpha with psili and perispomeni

Unicode	Character	1 2 3 4	Name
U1F0F	Ἇ Ἇ Ἇ	~ (A ~Ἁ	Greek capital letter alpha with dasia and perispomeni
U1F18	Ἐ Ἐ Ἐ	) E	Greek capital letter epsilon with psili
U1F19	Ἑ Ἑ Ἑ	(E	Greek capital letter epsilon with dasia
U1F1A	Ἒ Ἒ Ἒ	` ) E `Ἐ	Greek capital letter epsilon with psili and varia
U1F1B	Ἓ Ἓ Ἓ	` ( E `Ἑ	Greek capital letter epsilon with dasia and varia
U1F1C	Ἔ Ἔ Ἔ	') E 'Ἐ ´) E ´Ἐ	Greek capital letter epsilon with psili and oxia
U1F1D	Ἕ Ἕ Ἕ	' (E 'Ἑ ´ (E ´Ἑ	Greek capital letter epsilon with dasia and oxia
U1F28	Ἠ Ἠ Ἠ	) H	Greek capital letter eta with psili
U1F29	Ἡ Ἡ Ἡ	(H	Greek capital letter eta with dasia
U1F2A	Ἢ Ἢ Ἢ	` ) H `Ἠ	Greek capital letter eta with psili and varia
U1F2B	Ἣ Ἣ Ἣ	` ( H `Ἡ	Greek capital letter eta with dasia and varia
U1F2C	Ἤ Ἤ Ἤ	') H 'Ἠ ´) H ´Ἠ	Greek capital letter eta with psili and oxia
U1F2D	Ἥ Ἥ Ἥ	' (H 'Ἡ ´ (H ´Ἡ	Greek capital letter eta with dasia and oxia
U1F2E	Ἦ Ἦ Ἦ	~) H ~Ἠ	Greek capital letter eta with psili and perispomeni
U1F2F	Ἧ Ἧ Ἧ	~ (H ~Ἡ	Greek capital letter eta with dasia and perispomeni
U1F38	Ἰ Ἰ Ἰ	) I	Greek capital letter iota with psili
U1F39	Ἱ Ἱ Ἱ	(I	Greek capital letter iota with dasia
U1F3A	Ἲ Ἲ Ἲ	` ) I `Ἰ	Greek capital letter iota with psili and varia
U1F3B	Ἳ Ἳ Ἳ	` ( I `Ἱ	Greek capital letter iota with dasia and varia
U1F3C	Ἴ Ἴ Ἴ	') I 'Ἰ ´) I ´Ἰ	Greek capital letter iota with psili and oxia
U1F3D	Ἵ Ἵ Ἵ	' (I 'Ἱ ´ (I ´Ἱ	Greek capital letter iota with dasia and oxia
U1F3E	Ἶ Ἶ Ἶ	~) I ~Ἰ	Greek capital letter iota with psili and perispomeni

Unicode	Character	1 2 3 4	Name
U1F3F	῏Ι ῏Ι ῏Ι	~ (I ~῾I	Greek capital letter iota with dasia and perispomeni
U1F48	Ὀ Ὀ Ὀ	) O	Greek capital letter omicron with psili
U1F49	Ὁ Ὁ Ὁ	(O	Greek capital letter omicron with dasia
U1F4A	Ὂ Ὂ Ὂ	` ) O ` Ὀ	Greek capital letter omicron with psili and varia
U1F4B	Ὃ Ὃ Ὃ	` ( O ` Ὁ	Greek capital letter omicron with dasia and varia
U1F4C	Ὄ Ὄ Ὄ	') O ' Ὀ ´) O ´ Ὀ	Greek capital letter omicron with psili and oxia
U1F4D	Ὅ Ὅ Ὅ	' (O ' Ὁ ´ (O ´ Ὁ	Greek capital letter omicron with dasia and oxia
U1F59	Ὑ Ὑ Ὑ	(Y	Greek capital letter upsilon with dasia
U1F5B	Ὓ Ὓ Ὓ	` ( Y ` Ὑ	Greek capital letter upsilon with dasia and varia
U1F5D	Ὕ Ὕ Ὕ	' (Y ' Ὑ ´ (Y ´ Ὑ	Greek capital letter upsilon with dasia and oxia
U1F5F	Ὗ Ὗ Ὗ	~ (Y ~῾Y	Greek capital letter upsilon with dasia and perispomeni
U1F68	Ὠ Ὠ Ὠ	) Ω	Greek capital letter omega with psili
U1F69	Ὡ Ὡ Ὡ	(Ω	Greek capital letter omega with dasia
U1F6A	Ὢ Ὢ Ὢ	` ) Ω ` Ὠ	Greek capital letter omega with psili and varia
U1F6B	Ὣ Ὣ Ὣ	` ( Ω ` Ὡ	Greek capital letter omega with dasia and varia
U1F6C	Ὤ Ὤ Ὤ	') Ω ' Ὠ ´) Ω ´ Ὠ	Greek capital letter omega with psili and oxia
U1F6D	Ὥ Ὥ Ὥ	' (Ω ' Ὡ ´ (Ω ´ Ὡ	Greek capital letter omega with dasia and oxia
U1F6E	Ὦ Ὦ Ὦ	~) Ω ~ Ὠ	Greek capital letter omega with psili and perispomeni
U1F6F	Ὧ Ὧ Ὧ	~ (Ω ~ Ὡ	Greek capital letter omega with dasia and perispomeni
U1FB8	Ᾰ Ᾰ Ᾰ	U A b A	Greek capital letter alpha with vrachy
U1FB9	Ᾱ Ᾱ Ᾱ	_ A ¯ A	Greek capital letter alpha with macron
U1FBA	Ὰ Ὰ Ὰ	` A	Greek capital letter alpha with varia
U1FC8	Ὲ Ὲ Ὲ	` E	Greek capital letter epsilon with varia
U1FCA	Ὴ Ὴ Ὴ	` H	Greek capital letter eta with varia

Unicode	Character	1234	Name
U1FD8	Ῐ Ῐ Ῐ	UI bI	Greek capital letter iota with vrachy
U1FD9	Ῑ Ῑ Ῑ	_I ¯I	Greek capital letter iota with macron
U1FDA	Ὶ Ὶ Ὶ	`I	Greek capital letter iota with varia
U1FE8	Ῠ Ῠ Ῠ	UY bY	Greek capital letter upsilon with vrachy
U1FE9	Ῡ Ῡ Ῡ	_Y ¯Y	Greek capital letter upsilon with macron
U1FEA	Ὺ Ὺ Ὺ	`Y	Greek capital letter upsilon with varia
U1FEC	Ῥ Ῥ Ῥ	(P	Greek capital letter rho with dasia
U1FF8	Ὸ Ὸ Ὸ	`O	Greek capital letter omicron with varia
U1FFA	Ὼ Ὼ Ὼ	`Ω	Greek capital letter omega with varia

2.3 Letter, Titlecase (Lt)

Unicode	Character	1234	Name
U1F88	ᾈ ᾈ ᾈ	ι) A ιA	Greek capital letter alpha with psili and prosgegrammeni
U1F89	ᾉ ᾉ ᾉ	ι (A ιA	Greek capital letter alpha with dasia and prosgegrammeni
U1F8A	ᾊ ᾊ ᾊ	ι ` ) A ι `A ιA	Greek capital letter alpha with psili and varia and prosgegrammeni
U1F8B	ᾋ ᾋ ᾋ	ι ` ( A ι `A ιA	Greek capital letter alpha with dasia and varia and prosgegrammeni
U1F8C	ᾌ ᾌ ᾌ	ι ') A ι 'A ι ´) A ι ´A ιA	Greek capital letter alpha with psili and oxia and prosgegrammeni
U1F8D	ᾍ ᾍ ᾍ	ι ' (A ι 'A ι ´ (A ι ´A ιA	Greek capital letter alpha with dasia and oxia and prosgegrammeni
U1F8E	ᾎ ᾎ ᾎ	ι ~) A ι ~A ιA	Greek capital letter alpha with psili and perispomeni and prosgegrammeni
U1F8F	ᾏ ᾏ ᾏ	ι ~ (A ι ~A ιA	Greek capital letter alpha with dasia and perispomeni and prosgegrammeni
U1F98	ᾘ ᾘ ᾘ	ι) H ιH	Greek capital letter eta with psili and prosgegrammeni
U1F99	ᾙ ᾙ ᾙ	ι (H ιH	Greek capital letter eta with dasia and prosgegrammeni
U1F9A	ᾚ ᾚ ᾚ	ι ` ) H ι ` H ιH	Greek capital letter eta with psili and varia and prosgegrammeni

Unicode	Character	1 2 3 4	Name
U1F9B	Ἢ Ἢ ῃ	ι ` ( H   ι ` H ἱH	Greek capital letter eta with dasia and varia and prosgegrammeni
U1F9C	Ἤ Ἤ ῃ	ι ') H ι ' H ι ´) H ι ´ H ἰH	Greek capital letter eta with psili and oxia and prosgegrammeni
U1F9D	Ἥ Ἥ ῃ	ι ' (H ι ' H ι ´ (H ι ´ H ἱH	Greek capital letter eta with dasia and oxia and prosgegrammeni
U1F9E	Ἦ Ἦ ῃ	ι ~) H ι ~ H ι̃H	Greek capital letter eta with psili and perispomeni and prosgegrammeni
U1F9F	Ἧ Ἧ ῃ	ι ~ (H ι ~ H ι̃H	Greek capital letter eta with dasia and perispomeni and prosgegrammeni
U1FA8	Ὠ Ὠ ῳ	ι) Ω ἰΩ	Greek capital letter omega with psili and prosgegrammeni
U1FA9	Ὡ Ὡ ῳ	ι (Ω ἱΩ	Greek capital letter omega with dasia and prosgegrammeni
U1FAA	Ὢ Ὢ ῳ	ι ` ) Ω   ι ` Ω ἰΩ	Greek capital letter omega with psili and varia and prosgegrammeni
U1FAB	Ὣ Ὣ ῳ	ι ` ( Ω   ι ` Ω ἱΩ	Greek capital letter omega with dasia and varia and prosgegrammeni
U1FAC	Ὤ Ὤ ῳ	ι ') Ω ι ' Ω ι ´) Ω ι ´ Ω ἰΩ	Greek capital letter omega with psili and oxia and prosgegrammeni
U1FAD	Ὥ Ὥ ῳ	ι ' (Ω ι ' Ω ι ´ (Ω ι ´ Ω ἱΩ	Greek capital letter omega with dasia and oxia and prosgegrammeni
U1FAE	Ὦ Ὦ ῳ	ι ~) Ω ι ~ Ω ι̃Ω	Greek capital letter omega with psili and perispomeni and prosgegrammeni
U1FAF	Ὧ Ὧ ῳ	ι ~ (Ω ι ~ Ω ι̃Ω	Greek capital letter omega with dasia and perispomeni and prosgegrammeni
U1FBC	ΑΙ ΑΙ ῃ	ιA	Greek capital letter alpha with prosgegrammeni
U1FCC	ῌ ῌ ῃ	ιH	Greek capital letter eta with prosgegrammeni
U1FFC	ῼ ῼ ῳ	ιΩ	Greek capital letter omega with prosgegrammeni

2.4 Letter, Modifier (Lm)

Unicode	Character	1234	Name
U02B0	ʰ ʰ ʰ	^_h	Modifier letter small h
U02B1	ʱ ʱ ʱ	^_ɦ	Modifier letter small h with hook
U02B2	ʲ ʲ ʲ	^_j	Modifier letter small j
U02B3	ʳ ʳ ʳ	^_r	Modifier letter small r
U02B4	ʴ ʴ ʴ	^_ɹ	Modifier letter small turned r
U02B5	ʵ ʵ ʵ	^_ɻ	Modifier letter small turned r with hook
U02B6	ʶ ʶ ʶ	^_ʁ	Modifier letter small capital inverted r
U02B7	ʷ ʷ ʷ	^_w	Modifier letter small w
U02B8	ʸ ʸ ʸ	^_y	Modifier letter small y
U02C7	ˇ ˇ ˇ	<␣ ␣<	Caron
U02E0	ˠ ˠ ˠ	^_ɣ	Modifier letter small gamma
U02E1	ˡ ˡ ˡ	^_l	Modifier letter small l
U02E2	ˢ ˢ ˢ	^_s	Modifier letter small s
U02E3	ˣ ˣ ˣ	^_x	Modifier letter small x
U02E4	ˤ ˤ ˤ	^_ʕ	Modifier letter small reversed glottal stop
U2071	ⁱ ⁱ ⁱ	^_i	Superscript Latin small letter i
U207F	ⁿ ⁿ ⁿ	^_n	Superscript Latin small letter n

2.5 Letter, Other (Lo)

Unicode	Character	1234	Name
U00AA	ª ª ª	^_a	Feminine ordinal indicator
U00BA	º º º	^_o	Masculine ordinal indicator
U0622	آ آ	ٓ ا	Arabic letter alef with madda above
U0623	أ أ	ٔ ا	Arabic letter alef with hamza above
U0624	ؤ ؤ	ٔ و	Arabic letter waw with hamza above
U0625	إ إ	ٕ ا	Arabic letter alef with hamza below
U0626	ئ ئ	ٔ ى	Arabic letter yeh with hamza above
U06C0	ۀ ۀ	ٔ ه	Arabic letter heh with yeh above
U06C2	ۂ ۂ	ٔ ہ	Arabic letter heh goal with hamza above
U06D3	ۓ ۓ	ٔ ے	Arabic letter yeh barree with hamza above
U0929	ऩ ऩ	.न	Devanagari letter nnna
U0931	ऱ ऱ	.र	Devanagari letter rra
U0934	ऴ ऴ	.ळ	Devanagari letter llla
U0958	क़ क़	.क	Devanagari letter qa
U0959	ख़ ख़	.ख	Devanagari letter khha
U095A	ग़ ग़	.ग	Devanagari letter ghha
U095B	ज़ ज़	.ज	Devanagari letter za
U095C	ड़ ड़	.ड	Devanagari letter dddha
U095D	ढ़ ढ़	.ढ	Devanagari letter rha
U095E	फ़ फ़	.फ	Devanagari letter fa
U095F	य़ य़	.य	Devanagari letter yya
U09DC	ড় ড়	.ড	Bengali letter rra
U09DD	ঢ় ঢ়	.ঢ	Bengali letter rha
U09DF	য় য়	.য	Bengali letter yya
U0A33	ਲ਼ ਲ਼	.ਲ	Gurmukhi letter lla
U0A36	ਸ਼ ਸ਼	.ਸ	Gurmukhi letter sha

Unicode	Character	1 2 3 4	Name
U0A59	ਖ ਖ਼	. ਖ਼	Gurmukhi letter khha
U0A5A	ਗ ਗ਼	. ਗ਼	Gurmukhi letter ghha
U0A5B	ਜ ਜ਼	. ਜ਼	Gurmukhi letter za
U0A5E	ਫ ਫ਼	. ਫ਼	Gurmukhi letter fa
U0B5C	ଡ଼	. ଡ଼	Oriya letter rra
U0B5D	ଢ଼	. ଢ଼	Oriya letter rha
UFB1D	יִ	ִ י	Hebrew letter yod with hiriq
UFB1F	ײַ	ַ ײ	Hebrew ligature yiddish yod yod patah
UFB2A	שׁ	ׁ שׁ	Hebrew letter shin with shin dot
UFB2B	שׂ	ׂ שׂ	Hebrew letter shin with sin dot
UFB2C	שּׁ	ׁ ּ שׁ	Hebrew letter shin with dagesh and shin dot
UFB2D	שּׂ	ׂ ּ שׂ	Hebrew letter shin with dagesh and sin dot
UFB2E	אַ	ַ א	Hebrew letter alef with patah
UFB2F	אָ	ָ א	Hebrew letter alef with qamats
UFB30	אּ	ּ א	Hebrew letter alef with mapiq
UFB31	בּ	ּ ב	Hebrew letter bet with dagesh
UFB32	גּ	ּ ג	Hebrew letter gimel with dagesh
UFB33	דּ	ּ ד	Hebrew letter dalet with dagesh
UFB34	הּ	ּ ה	Hebrew letter he with mapiq
UFB35	וּ	ּ ו	Hebrew letter vav with dagesh
UFB36	זּ	ּ ז	Hebrew letter zayin with dagesh
UFB38	טּ	ּ ט	Hebrew letter tet with dagesh
UFB39	יּ	ּ י	Hebrew letter yod with dagesh
UFB3A	ךּ	ּ ך	Hebrew letter final kaf with dagesh
UFB3B	כּ	ּ כ	Hebrew letter kaf with dagesh
UFB3C	לּ	ּ ל	Hebrew letter lamed with dagesh
UFB3E	מּ	ּ מ	Hebrew letter mem with dagesh
UFB40	נּ	ּ נ	Hebrew letter nun with dagesh
UFB41	סּ	ּ ס	Hebrew letter samekh with dagesh
UFB43	ףּ	ּ ף	Hebrew letter final pe with dagesh
UFB44	פּ	ּ פ	Hebrew letter pe with dagesh
UFB46	צּ	ּ צ	Hebrew letter tsadi with dagesh
UFB47	קּ	ּ ק	Hebrew letter qof with dagesh
UFB48	רּ	ּ ר	Hebrew letter resh with dagesh
UFB49	שּ	ּ ש	Hebrew letter shin with dagesh
UFB4A	תּ	ּ ת	Hebrew letter tav with dagesh
UFB4B	וֹ	ֹ ו	Hebrew letter vav with holam
UFB4C	בֿ	ֿ ב	Hebrew letter bet with rafe
UFB4D	כֿ	ֿ כ	Hebrew letter kaf with rafe
UFB4E	פֿ	ֿ פ	Hebrew letter pe with rafe

2.6 Punctuation, Dash (Pd)

Unicode	Character	1234	Name
U2013	– – –	– – .	En dash
U2014	— — –	– – –	Em dash

2.7 Punctuation, Open (Ps)

Unicode	Character			1 2 3 4	Name
U005B	[	[	[	((	Left square bracket
U007B	{	{	{	(−	Left curly bracket
				− (	
U201A	‚	‚	‚	' ‚	Single low-9 quotation mark
				‚ '	
U201E	„	„	„	" ‚	Double low-9 quotation mark
				‚ "	
U207D	⁽	⁽	⁽	^ (	Superscript left parenthesis
U208D	₍	₍	₍	_ (	Subscript left parenthesis

2.8 Punctuation, Close (Pe)

Unicode	Character			1 2 3 4	Name
U005D	]	]	]	))	Right square bracket
U007D	}	}	}	) −	Right curly bracket
				−)	
U207E	⁾	⁾	⁾	^)	Superscript right parenthesis
U208E	₎	₎	₎	_)	Subscript right parenthesis

2.9 Punctuation, Initial quote (Pi)

Unicode	Character			1 2 3 4	Name
U00AB	«	«	«	< <	Left-pointing double angle quotation mark
U2018	'	'	'	' <	Left single quotation mark
				< '	
U201C	"	"	"	" <	Left double quotation mark
				< "	
U2039	‹	‹	‹	. <	Single left-pointing angle quotation mark

2.10 Punctuation, Final quote (Pf)

Unicode	Character			1 2 3 4	Name
U00BB	»	»	»	> >	Right-pointing double angle quotation mark
U2019	'	'	'	' >	Right single quotation mark
				> '	
U201D	"	"	"	" >	Right double quotation mark
				> "	
U203A	›	›	›	. >	Single right-pointing angle quotation mark

2.11 Punctuation, Other (Po)

Unicode	Character			1234		Name
U0023	#	#	#	+ +		Number sign
U0027	'	'	'	' ␣		Apostrophe
				␣ '		
U0040	@	@	@	A T		Commercial at
U005C	\	\	\	/ /		Reverse solidus
				/ <		
				< /		
U00A1	¡	¡	¡	! !		Inverted exclamation mark
U00A7	§	§	§	O S		Section sign
				S !		
				S O		
				o s		
				s !		
				s o		
				п а		
U00B6	¶	¶	¶	P !		Pilcrow sign
				P P		
				p !		
U00B7	·	·	·	. −		Middle dot
				. ^		
				^ .		
U00BF	¿	¿	¿	? ?		Inverted question mark
U2022	•	•	•	. =		Bullet
U2026	...	...	...	. .		Horizontal ellipsis
U2030	‰	‰	‰	% o		Per mille sign
U203D	‽	‽	‽	! ?		Interrobang
U2E18	⸘	⸘	⸘	? !		Inverted interrobang

2.12 Number, Other (No)

Unicode	Character			1234	Name
U00B2	^{2}	^{2}	^{2}	2 ^	Superscript two
				^ 2	
U00B3	^{3}	^{3}	^{3}	3 ^	Superscript three
				^ 3	
U00B9	^{1}	^{1}	^{1}	1 ^	Superscript one
				^ 1	
U00BC	¼	¼	¼	1 4	Vulgar fraction one quarter
U00BD	½	½	½	1 2	Vulgar fraction one half
U00BE	¾	¾	¾	3 4	Vulgar fraction three quarters
U2070	^{0}	^{0}	^{0}	^ 0	Superscript zero
U2074	^{4}	^{4}	^{4}	^ 4	Superscript four
U2075	^{5}	^{5}	^{5}	^ 5	Superscript five
U2076	^{6}	^{6}	^{6}	^ 6	Superscript six
U2077	^{7}	^{7}	^{7}	^ 7	Superscript seven
U2078	^{8}	^{8}	^{8}	^ 8	Superscript eight
U2079	^{9}	^{9}	^{9}	^ 9	Superscript nine
U2080	$_0$	$_0$	$_0$	_ 0	Subscript zero

Unicode	Character	1 2 3 4	Name
U2081	1 1 1	_1	Subscript one
U2082	2 2 2	_2	Subscript two
U2083	3 3 3	_3	Subscript three
U2084	4 4 4	_4	Subscript four
U2085	5 5 5	_5	Subscript five
U2086	6 6 6	_6	Subscript six
U2087	7 7 7	_7	Subscript seven
U2088	8 8 8	_8	Subscript eight
U2089	9 9 9	_9	Subscript nine
U2150	1/7	17	Vulgar fraction one seventh
U2151	1/9	19	Vulgar fraction one ninth
U2152	1/10	110	Vulgar fraction one tenth
U2153	1/3 1/3 1/3	13	Vulgar fraction one third
U2154	2/3 2/3 2/3	23	Vulgar fraction two thirds
U2155	1/5 1/5 1/5	15	Vulgar fraction one fifth
U2156	2/5 2/5 2/5	25	Vulgar fraction two fifths
U2157	3/5 3/5 3/5	35	Vulgar fraction three fifths
U2158	4/5 4/5 4/5	45	Vulgar fraction four fifths
U2159	1/6 1/6 1/6	16	Vulgar fraction one sixth
U215A	5/6 5/6 5/6	56	Vulgar fraction five sixths
U215B	1/8 1/8 1/8	18	Vulgar fraction one eighth
U215C	3/8 3/8 3/8	38	Vulgar fraction three eighths
U215D	5/8 5/8 5/8	58	Vulgar fraction five eighths
U215E	7/8 7/8 7/8	78	Vulgar fraction seven eighths
U2189	0/3	03	Vulgar fraction zero thirds
U2460	① ① ①	(1)	Circled digit one
U2461	② ② ②	(2)	Circled digit two
U2462	③ ③ ③	(3)	Circled digit three
U2463	④ ④ ④	(4)	Circled digit four
U2464	⑤ ⑤ ⑤	(5)	Circled digit five
U2465	⑥ ⑥ ⑥	(6)	Circled digit six
U2466	⑦ ⑦ ⑦	(7)	Circled digit seven
U2467	⑧ ⑧ ⑧	(8)	Circled digit eight
U2468	⑨ ⑨ ⑨	(9)	Circled digit nine
U2469	⑩ ⑩	(10)	Circled number ten
U246A	⑪ ⑪	(11)	Circled number eleven
U246B	⑫ ⑫	(12)	Circled number twelve
U246C	⑬ ⑬	(13)	Circled number thirteen
U246D	⑭ ⑭	(14)	Circled number fourteen
U246E	⑮ ⑮	(15)	Circled number fifteen
U246F	⑯ ⑯	(16)	Circled number sixteen
U2470	⑰ ⑰	(17)	Circled number seventeen
U2471	⑱ ⑱	(18)	Circled number eighteen
U2472	⑲ ⑲	(19)	Circled number nineteen
U2473	⑳ ⑳	(20)	Circled number twenty
U24EA	⓪ ⓪	(0)	Circled digit zero

2.13   Symbol, Math (Sm)

Unicode	Character			1 2 3 4	Name
U007C	|	|	|	/ ^	Vertical line
				LV	
				VL	
				^ /	
				lv	
				vl	
U007E	~	~	~	— ␣	Tilde
				~ ␣	
				␣ —	
				␣ ~	
U00AC	¬	¬	¬	, —	Not sign
				— ,	
U00B1	±	±	±	+ —	Plus-minus sign
				— +	
U00D7	×	×	×	x x	Multiplication sign
U00F7	÷	÷	÷	— :	Division sign
				: —	
U207A	+	+	+	^ +	Superscript plus sign
U207B	-	-	-	^ —	Superscript minus
U207C	=	=	=	^ =	Superscript equals sign
U208A	+	+	+	_ +	Subscript plus sign
U208B	-	-	-	_ —	Subscript minus
U208C	=	=	=	_ =	Subscript equals sign
U2190	←	←	←	< —	Leftwards arrow
U2192	→	→	→	— >	Rightwards arrow
U219A		↚	↚	/ →	Leftwards arrow with stroke
U219B		↛	↛	/ ←	Rightwards arrow with stroke
U21AE		↮	↮	/ ↔	Left right arrow with stroke
U2204	∄	∄	∄	∃ /	There does not exist
U2205	∅	∅	∅	{ }	Empty set
U2209	∉	∉	∉	∈ /	Not an element of
U220C	∌	∌	∌	∋ /	Does not contain as member
U221A	√	√	√	/ v	Square root
				v /	
U221E	∞	∞	∞	8 8	Infinity
U2224	∤	∤	∤	| /	Does not divide
U2226	∦	∦	∦	|| /	Not parallel to
U2234	∴	∴	∴	: .	Therefore
U2235	∵	∵	∵	. :	Because
U2241	≁	≁	≁	~ /	Not tilde
U2244	≄	≄	≄	≃ /	Not asymptotically equal to
U2247	≇	≇	≇	≈ /	Neither approximately nor actually equal to
U2249	≉	≉	≉	≈ /	Not almost equal to
U2260	≠	≠	≠	/ =	Not equal to
				= /	
U2261	≡	≡	≡	= _	Identical to
U2262	≢	≢	≢	_ ≠	Not identical to
				≠ _	
				≡ /	

Unicode	Character			1 2 3 4	Name
U2264	≤	≤	≤	<=	Less-than or equal to
				<_	
				_<	
U2265	≥	≥	≥	>=	Greater-than or equal to
				>_	
				_>	
U226D	≭	≭	≭	≍/	Not equivalent to
U226E	≮	≮	≮	</	Not less-than
				</	
U226F	≯	≯	≯	>/	Not greater-than
				>/	
U2270	≰	≰	≰	≤/	Neither less-than nor equal to
U2271	≱	≱	≱	≥/	Neither greater-than nor equal to
U2274		≴	≴	≲/	Neither less-than nor equivalent to
U2275		≵	≵	≳/	Neither greater-than nor equivalent to
U2278		≸	≸	≶/	Neither less-than nor greater-than
U2279		≹	≹	≷/	Neither greater-than nor less-than
U2280	⊀	⊀	⊀	</	Does not precede
U2281	⊁	⊁	⊁	>/	Does not succeed
U2284	⊄	⊄	⊄	⊂/	Not a subset of
U2285	⊅	⊅	⊅	⊃/	Not a superset of
U2286	⊆	⊆	⊆	_⊂	Subset of or equal to
				⊂_	
U2287	⊇	⊇	⊇	_⊃	Superset of or equal to
				⊃_	
U2288	⊈	⊈	⊈	⊆/	Neither a subset of nor equal to
U2289	⊉	⊉	⊉	⊇/	Neither a superset of nor equal to
U2296	⊖	⊖	⊖	−O	Circled minus
				O−	
U2299	⊙	⊙	⊙	.O	Circled dot operator
				O.	
U22AC		⊬	⊬	⊢/	Does not prove
U22AD		⊭	⊭	⊨/	Not true
U22AE		⊮	⊮	⊩/	Does not force
U22AF		⊯	⊯	⊫/	Negated double vertical bar double right turnstile
U22C4		◇	•	<>	Diamond operator
				><	
				∧∨	
				∨∧	
U22E0	⋠	⋠	⋠	≼/	Does not precede or equal
U22E1	⋡	⋡	⋡	≽/	Does not succeed or equal
U22E2	⋢	⋢	⋢	⊑/	Not square image of or equal to
U22E3	⋣	⋣	⋣	⊒/	Not square original of or equal to
U22EA		⋪	⋪	◁/	Not normal subgroup of
U22EB		⋫	⋫	▷/	Does not contain as normal subgroup
U22EC		⋬	⋬	⊴/	Not normal subgroup of or equal to
U22ED		⋭	⋭	⊵/	Does not contain as normal subgroup or equal
U266F	♯	♯	♯	##	Music sharp sign

2.14 Symbol, Currency (Sc)

Unicode	Character	1 2 3 4	Name
U00A2	¢ ¢ ¢	/c C| c/ c| |C |c	Cent sign
U00A3	£ £ £	-L -l L- l-	Pound sign
U00A4	¤ ¤ ¤	OX Ox XO Xo oX ox xO xo	Currency sign
U00A5	¥ ¥ ¥	-Y -y =Y =y Y- Y= y- y=	Yen sign
U20A0	₠ ₠	CE	Euro-currency sign
U20A1	₡ ₡ ₡	/C C/	Colon sign
U20A2	₢ ₢ ₢	Cr	Cruzeiro sign
U20A3	₣ ₣ ₣	Fr	French franc sign
U20A4	₤ ₤ ₤	=L L=	Lira sign
U20A5	₥ ₥ ₥	/m m/	Mill sign
U20A6	₦ ₦ ₦	=N N=	Naira sign
U20A7	₧ ₧ ₧	Pt	Peseta sign
U20A8	₨ ₨ ₨	Rs	Rupee sign
U20A9	₩ ₩ ₩	=W W=	Won sign
U20AB	₫ ₫ ₫	=d d=	Dong sign

Unicode	Character	1234	Name
U20AC	€ € €	=C	Euro sign
		=E	
		=c	
		=e	
		=E	
		=C	
		C=	
		E=	
		c=	
		e=	
		E=	
		C=	

2.15 Symbol, Other (So)

Unicode	Character	1234	Name
U00A6	¦ ¦ ¦	! ^	Broken bar
U00A9	© © ©	CO	Copyright sign
		Co	
		OC	
		Oc	
		oC	
		oc	
U00AE	® ® ®	OR	Registered sign
		Or	
		RO	
		oR	
		or	
U00B0	° ° °	*0	Degree sign
		0*	
		oo	
U1D15E	♩	o|	Musical symbol half note
U1D15F	♩	•|	Musical symbol quarter note
U1D160	♪	♩♪	Musical symbol eighth note
U1D161	♫	♩♪	Musical symbol sixteenth note
U1D162	♬	♩♪	Musical symbol thirty-second note
U1D163	♬	♩♪	Musical symbol sixty-fourth note
U1D164	♬	♩♪	Musical symbol one hundred twenty-eighth note
U1D1BB	↓	o|	Musical symbol minima
U1D1BC	↓	•|	Musical symbol minima black
U1D1BD	♪	↓♪	Musical symbol semiminima white
U1D1BE	♪	↓♪	Musical symbol semiminima black
U1D1BF	♪	↓♪	Musical symbol fusa white
U1D1C0	♪	↓♪	Musical symbol fusa black
U2116	№ № №	NO	Numero sign
		No	
		HO	
		Ho	

Unicode	Character	1 2 3 4	Name
U2120	SM SM ɴᴍ	SM	Service mark
		Sm	
		sM	
		sm	
U2122	TM TM ᴛᴍ	TM	Trade mark sign
		Tm	
		tM	
		tm	
U2300	Ø ⊘ ø	di	Diameter sign
U2336	⌶	T⊥	APL functional symbol i-beam
		⊥T	
U2337	⌷	[ ]	APL functional symbol squish quad
		] [	
U2338	⌸	=□	APL functional symbol quad equal
		□=	
U2339	⌹	÷□	APL functional symbol quad divide
		□÷	
U233A	⌺	·□	APL functional symbol quad diamond
		□·	
U233B	⌻	○□	APL functional symbol quad jot
		□○	
U233C	⌼	O□	APL functional symbol quad circle
		□O	
U233D	⌽	O|	APL functional symbol circle stile
		|O	
U233E	⌾	O○	APL functional symbol circle jot
		○O	
U233F	⌿	−/	APL functional symbol slash bar
		/−	
U2340	⍀	−\	APL functional symbol backslash bar
		\−	
U2341	⍁	/□	APL functional symbol quad slash
		□/	
U2342	⍂	\□	APL functional symbol quad backslash
		□\	
U2343	⍃	<□	APL functional symbol quad less-than
		□<	
U2344	⍄	>□	APL functional symbol quad greater-than
		□>	
U2345	⍅	|←	APL functional symbol leftwards vane
		←|	
U2346	⍆	|→	APL functional symbol rightwards vane
		→|	
U2347	⍇ ⍇	←□	APL functional symbol quad leftwards arrow
		□←	
U2348	⍈ ⍈	→□	APL functional symbol quad rightwards arrow
		□→	
U2349	⍉	O\	APL functional symbol circle backslash
		\O	
U234A	⊥	⊥_	APL functional symbol down tack underbar
		_⊥	

Unicode	Character	1 2 3 4	Name
U234B	⍋	| △ △ |	APL functional symbol delta stile
U234C	⍌	∨▢ ▢∨	APL functional symbol quad down caret
U234D	⍍	△▢ ▢△	APL functional symbol quad delta
U234E	⍎	⊥○ ○⊥	APL functional symbol down tack jot
U234F	⍏	− ↑ ↑ −	APL functional symbol upwards vane
U2350	⍐ ⍐	↑▢ ▢↑	APL functional symbol quad upwards arrow
U2351	⍑	⊤‾ ‾⊤	APL functional symbol up tack overbar
U2352	⍒	| ∇ ∇ |	APL functional symbol del stile
U2353	⍓	∧▢ ▢∧	APL functional symbol quad up caret
U2354	⍔	∇▢ ▢∇	APL functional symbol quad del
U2355	⍕	⊤○ ○⊤	APL functional symbol up tack jot
U2356	⍖	− ↓ ↓ −	APL functional symbol downwards vane
U2357	⍗ ⍗	↓▢ ▢↓	APL functional symbol quad downwards arrow
U2358	⍘	_'	APL functional symbol quote underbar
U2359	⍙	_△ △_	APL functional symbol delta underbar
U235A	⍚	◆_ _◆	APL functional symbol diamond underbar
U235B	⍛	_○ ○_	APL functional symbol jot underbar
U235C	⍜	○_ _○	APL functional symbol circle underbar
U235D	⍝	○∩ ∩○	APL functional symbol up shoe jot
U235E	⍞ ⍞	'▢ ▢'	APL functional symbol quote quad
U235F	⍟	*○ ○*	APL functional symbol circle star
U2360	⍠	:▢ ▢:	APL functional symbol quad colon
U2361	⍡	⊤¨ ¨⊤	APL functional symbol up tack diaeresis
U2362	⍢	¨∇ ∇¨	APL functional symbol del diaeresis
U2363	⍣	*¨ ¨*	APL functional symbol star diaeresis
U2364	⍤	¨○ ○¨	APL functional symbol jot diaeresis

Unicode	Character	1 2 3 4	Name
U2365	⍥	O⋅⋅ ⋅⋅O	APL functional symbol circle diaeresis
U2366	⍦	∪| |∪	APL functional symbol down shoe stile
U2367	⍧	|⊂ ⊂|	APL functional symbol left shoe stile
U2368	⍨	~⋅⋅	APL functional symbol tilde diaeresis
U2369	⍩	>⋅⋅ ⋅⋅>	APL functional symbol greater-than diaeresis
U236B	⍫	~∇ ∇~	APL functional symbol del tilde
U236C	⍬	0~ ~0	APL functional symbol zilde
U236D	⍭	|~ ~|	APL functional symbol stile tilde
U236E	⍮	;_	APL functional symbol semicolon underbar
U236F	⍯	≠□ □≠	APL functional symbol quad not equal
U2370	⍰ ⍰ ⍰	?□ □?	APL functional symbol quad question
U2371	⍱	~∨ ∨~	APL functional symbol down caret tilde
U2372	⍲	~∧ ∧~	APL functional symbol up caret tilde
U2376	⍶	α_ _α	APL functional symbol alpha underbar
U2377	⍷	∊_ _∊	APL functional symbol epsilon underbar
U2378	⍸	_ι ι_	APL functional symbol iota underbar
U2379	⍹	_ω ω_	APL functional symbol omega underbar
U24B6	Ⓐ Ⓐ	(A) OA	Circled Latin capital letter a
U24B7	Ⓑ Ⓑ	(B)	Circled Latin capital letter b
U24B8	Ⓒ Ⓒ	(C)	Circled Latin capital letter c
U24B9	Ⓓ Ⓓ	(D)	Circled Latin capital letter d
U24BA	Ⓔ Ⓔ	(E)	Circled Latin capital letter e
U24BB	Ⓕ Ⓕ	(F)	Circled Latin capital letter f
U24BC	Ⓖ Ⓖ	(G)	Circled Latin capital letter g
U24BD	Ⓗ Ⓗ	(H)	Circled Latin capital letter h
U24BE	Ⓘ Ⓘ	(I)	Circled Latin capital letter i
U24BF	Ⓙ Ⓙ	(J)	Circled Latin capital letter j
U24C0	Ⓚ Ⓚ	(K)	Circled Latin capital letter k
U24C1	Ⓛ Ⓛ	(L)	Circled Latin capital letter l
U24C2	Ⓜ Ⓜ	(M)	Circled Latin capital letter m
U24C3	Ⓝ Ⓝ	(N)	Circled Latin capital letter n
U24C4	Ⓞ Ⓞ	(O)	Circled Latin capital letter o
U24C5	Ⓟ Ⓟ	(P)	Circled Latin capital letter p
U24C6	Ⓠ Ⓠ	(Q)	Circled Latin capital letter q
U24C7	Ⓡ Ⓡ	(R)	Circled Latin capital letter r
U24C8	Ⓢ Ⓢ	(S)	Circled Latin capital letter s

Unicode	Character	1 2 3 4	Name
U24C9	Ⓣ Ⓣ	(T)	Circled Latin capital letter t
U24CA	Ⓤ Ⓤ	(U)	Circled Latin capital letter u
U24CB	Ⓥ Ⓥ	(V)	Circled Latin capital letter v
U24CC	Ⓦ Ⓦ	(W)	Circled Latin capital letter w
U24CD	Ⓧ Ⓧ	(X)	Circled Latin capital letter x
U24CE	Ⓨ Ⓨ	(Y)	Circled Latin capital letter y
U24CF	Ⓩ Ⓩ	(Z)	Circled Latin capital letter z
U24D0	ⓐ ⓐ	(a)	Circled Latin small letter a
U24D1	ⓑ ⓑ	(b)	Circled Latin small letter b
U24D2	ⓒ ⓒ	(c)	Circled Latin small letter c
U24D3	ⓓ ⓓ	(d)	Circled Latin small letter d
U24D4	ⓔ ⓔ	(e)	Circled Latin small letter e
U24D5	ⓕ ⓕ	(f)	Circled Latin small letter f
U24D6	ⓖ ⓖ	(g)	Circled Latin small letter g
U24D7	ⓗ ⓗ	(h)	Circled Latin small letter h
U24D8	ⓘ ⓘ	(i)	Circled Latin small letter i
U24D9	ⓙ ⓙ	(j)	Circled Latin small letter j
U24DA	ⓚ ⓚ	(k)	Circled Latin small letter k
U24DB	ⓛ ⓛ	(l)	Circled Latin small letter l
U24DC	ⓜ ⓜ	(m)	Circled Latin small letter m
U24DD	ⓝ ⓝ	(n)	Circled Latin small letter n
U24DE	ⓞ ⓞ	(o)	Circled Latin small letter o
U24DF	ⓟ ⓟ	(p)	Circled Latin small letter p
U24E0	ⓠ ⓠ	(q)	Circled Latin small letter q
U24E1	ⓡ ⓡ	(r)	Circled Latin small letter r
U24E2	ⓢ ⓢ	(s)	Circled Latin small letter s
U24E3	ⓣ ⓣ	(t)	Circled Latin small letter t
U24E4	ⓤ ⓤ	(u)	Circled Latin small letter u
U24E5	ⓥ ⓥ	(v)	Circled Latin small letter v
U24E6	ⓦ ⓦ	(w)	Circled Latin small letter w
U24E7	ⓧ ⓧ	(x)	Circled Latin small letter x
U24E8	ⓨ ⓨ	(y)	Circled Latin small letter y
U24E9	ⓩ ⓩ	(z)	Circled Latin small letter z
U262D	☭ ☭	CCCP	Hammer and sickle
U2639	☹ ☹ ☹	: (	White frowning face
U263A	☺ ☺ ☺	:)	White smiling face
U2665	♥ ♥ ♥	<3	Black heart suit
U2669	♩ ♩ ♩	#q	Quarter note
U266A	♪ ♪ ♪	#e	Eighth note
U266B	♫ ♫ ♫	#E	Beamed eighth notes
U266C	♬ ♬ ♬	#S	Beamed sixteenth notes
U266D	♭ ♭ ♭	#b	Music flat sign
U266E	♮ ♮ ♮	#f	Music natural sign

2.16   Symbol, Modifier (Sk)

Unicode	Character	1 2 3 4	Name
U005E	^ ^ ^	>␣	Circumflex accent
		^␣	
		␣>	
		␣^	

Unicode	Character	1 2 3 4	Name
U0060	` ` `	` ␣ ␣ `	Grave accent
U00A8	¨ ¨ ¨	" "	Diaeresis
U00AF	‾ ‾ ‾	_ ^ ^ _ _ ^ ‾	Macron
U00B4	´ ´ ´	' '	Acute accent
U00B8	¸ ¸ ¸	/ / / ␣ ␣ /	Cedilla
U02D8	˘ ˘ ˘	(␣ ␣ (	Breve
U0385	΅ ΅ ΅	' " ␣ ¨ ' ¨ ´	Greek dialytika tonos
U1FC1	῁ ῁ ῁	¨ ~	Greek dialytika and perispomeni
U1FCD	῍ ῍ ῍	' `	Greek psili and varia
U1FCE	῎ ῎ ῎	' ' ' ´	Greek psili and oxia
U1FCF	῏ ῏ ῏	' ~	Greek psili and perispomeni
U1FDD	῝ ῝ ῝	' `	Greek dasia and varia
U1FDE	῞ ῞ ῞	' ' ' ´	Greek dasia and oxia
U1FDF	῟ ῟ ῟	' ~	Greek dasia and perispomeni
U1FED	῭ ῭ ῭	¨ `	Greek dialytika and varia

2.17 Mark, Non-Spacing (Mn)

Unicode	Character	1 2 3 4	Name
U0344	̈́ ̈́ ̈́	" ' " ´	Combining Greek dialytika tonos

2.18 Separator, Space (Zs)

Unicode	Character	1 2 3 4	Name
U00A0		␣ ␣	No-break space
U2008		␣ .	Punctuation space

2.19 Other, Format (Cf)

Unicode	Character	1 2 3 4	Name
U00AD	- - –	– – ␣	Soft hyphen

2.20 Diacritics, Combining (Dc)

Unicode	Character	1 2 3 4	Name
U0410 U0300	À À À	`` `A ``	Cyrillic capital letter a with combining grave accent
U0410 U0301	Á Á Á	`` 'A `` `` ´A ``	Cyrillic capital letter a with combining acute accent
U0410 U030F	Ӑ Ӑ Ӑ	`` ``A ``	Cyrillic capital letter a with combining double grave accent
U0415 U0301	É É É	`` 'E `` `` ´E ``	Cyrillic capital letter ie with combining acute accent
U0415 U030F	Ӗ Ӗ Ӗ	`` ``E ``	Cyrillic capital letter ie with combining double grave accent
U0418 U0301	Ѝ Ѝ Ѝ	`` 'И `` `` ´И ``	Cyrillic capital letter i with combining acute accent
U0418 U030F	Ӥ Ӥ Ӥ	`` ``И ``	Cyrillic capital letter i with combining double grave accent
U041E U0300	Ò Ò Ò	`` `O ``	Cyrillic capital letter o with combining grave accent
U041E U0301	Ó Ó Ó	`` 'O `` `` ´O ``	Cyrillic capital letter o with combining acute accent
U041E U030F	Ӧ Ӧ Ӧ	`` ``O ``	Cyrillic capital letter o with combining double grave accent
U0420 U0300	Р̀ Р̀ Р̀	`` `P ``	Cyrillic capital letter er with combining grave accent
U0420 U0301	Р́ Р́ Р́	`` 'P `` `` ´P ``	Cyrillic capital letter er with combining acute accent
U0420 U030F	Р̏ Р̏ Р̏	`` ``P ``	Cyrillic capital letter er with combining double grave accent
U0423 U0300	У̀ У̀ У̀	`` `y ``	Cyrillic capital letter u with combining grave accent
U0423 U0301	У́ У́ У́	`` 'y `` `` ´y ``	Cyrillic capital letter u with combining acute accent
U0423 U030F	У̏ У̏ У̏	`` ``y ``	Cyrillic capital letter u with combining double grave accent
U0430 U0300	à à à	`` `a ``	Cyrillic small letter a with combining grave accent
U0430 U0301	á á á	`` 'a `` `` ´a ``	Cyrillic small letter a with combining acute accent
U0430 U030F	ӑ ӑ ӑ	`` ``a ``	Cyrillic small letter a with combining double grave accent
U0435 U0301	é é é	`` 'e `` `` ´e ``	Cyrillic small letter ie with combining acute accent
U0435 U030F	ӗ ӗ ӗ	`` ``e ``	Cyrillic small letter ie with combining double grave accent
U0438 U0301	ѝ ѝ ѝ	`` 'и `` `` ´и ``	Cyrillic small letter i with combining acute accent
U0438 U030F	ӥ ӥ ӥ	`` ``и ``	Cyrillic small letter i with combining double grave accent
U043E U0300	ò ò ò	`` `o ``	Cyrillic small letter o with combining grave accent
U043E U0301	ó ó ó	`` 'o `` `` ´o ``	Cyrillic small letter o with combining acute accent
U043E U030F	ӧ ӧ ӧ	`` ``o ``	Cyrillic small letter o with combining double grave accent
U0440 U0300	р̀ р̀ р̀	`` `p ``	Cyrillic small letter er with combining grave accent
U0440 U0301	р́ р́ р́	`` 'p `` `` ´p ``	Cyrillic small letter er with combining acute accent
U0440 U030F	р̏ р̏ р̏	`` ``p ``	Cyrillic small letter er with combining double grave accent
U0443 U0300	у̀ у̀ у̀	`` `y ``	Cyrillic small letter u with combining grave accent
U0443 U0301	у́ у́ у́	`` 'y `` `` ´y ``	Cyrillic small letter u with combining acute accent
U0443 U030F	у̏ у̏ у̏	`` ``y ``	Cyrillic small letter u with combining double grave accent

Chapter 3

ASCII Compose Sequence Matrix

This chapter offers a matrix proving a practical overview for looking up two-key compose sequences and resulting characters. Two-key compose sequences are often used and relatively easy to remember. These sequences can be created with keys found on most QWERTY-like keyboards.

The keys specifically needed to enter these sequences are also the first 95 printable characters of Unicode. That is, the keys representing lower and upper case letters of the Latin alphabet [a] to [Z], numerals [0] to [9], mathematical symbols such as [+] and [=] and punctuation marks such as [?] and ["]. This range is identical to all of the printable ASCII characters which were in use at the time most QWERTY-like keyboards were first designed.

Two-key compose sequences made from ASCII and resulting characters are documented in a matrix that has been divided over the next four pages. Keys along the top and bottom of the matrix are the first and keys along the left and right side are the second in two-key sequences. The resulting character is found in the cell where there respective column and row for these two keys intersect. Note that ␣ is used to represent the space bar [_____]. The characters q and Q have been omitted in several places in the matrix because no ASCII compose sequences containing these two characters exist.

For every compose sequence the exact order of the sequence is important. Originally, the order of the sequences was usually a symbol followed by a letter for characters with diacritics. One example is [⟁] [ˋ] [a] for à. Later the reverse sequence was supported as well because in most language one speaks or thinks of *a-acute* rather than *acute-a*. Hence mirrored or symmetric sequences such as [⟁] [a] [ˋ] were defined which are easier to reproduce in order to get, in this case, à.

Symbolic characters can have symmetric compose sequences too but it is usually up to the user which is easier to remember and use. See for example [⟁] [S] [O] and [⟁] [O] [S] for §. Obviously the compose sequence [⟁] [1] [2] for ½ has no viable reversed sequence as alternative.

Three-key and four-key compose sequences, which cannot be represented in this two-dimensional matrix, need to begin with an unassigned two-key sequence. These two-key sequences need one or more characters in order to determine which three-key or four-key compose sequence is requested. The number of possible three-key or four-key compose sequences is shown in the matrix in white on a gray background for the two-key sequence with which they begin. An example is [⟁] [b] [,] which will need an extra character to determine which of the two available three-key sequences beginning with this two-key sequence is intended. This is either an [e] to result in ę̆ or an [E] to result in Ę̆. The exact three-key and four-key sequences can be found in the previous and next chapter.

A poster containing a unified single large matrix with extra rows and columns is available by the same publisher of this reference guide. Each Unicode character is shown in the serif font from of the GNU FreeFont family.

3.1 Compose Sequence Matrix (top left)

↵	a	b	c	d	e	f	g	h	i	j	k	l	m	n	o	p	r	s	t	u	v	w	x	y	z	A	B	C	D	E	F	G	H	I	J	K	L	M	N	O	P	Q	R	↵
'	á		ć		é				í			Í		ń	ó		ŕ	ś		ú				ý	ź	Á		Ć		É				Í			Ĺ		Ń	Ó			Ŕ	'
`	à				è				ì						ò					ù						À				È				Ì						Ò				`
"	ä				ë				ï						ö					ü				ÿ		Ä				Ë				Ï						Ö				"
^	â				ê				î						ô					û		ŵ		ŷ		Â				Ê				Î						Ô				^
_	ā				ē				ī						ō					ū						Ā				Ē				Ī						Ō				_
~	ã								ĩ					ñ	õ					ũ						Ã								Ĩ						Ñ	Õ			~
/			¢									ł	ḿ		ø				ŧ	µ	√							¢									Ł			Ø				/
,	ą		ç	ḑ	ę		ģ	ḩ	i		ķ	ļ		ņ			ŗ	ş	ţ	ų						Ą		Ç	Ḑ	Ę		Ģ	Ḩ	Į		Ķ	Ļ		Ņ				Ŗ	,
.		ḃ	ċ	ḋ	ė	ḟ	ġ		ı				ṁ			ṗ		ś	ṫ						ż		Ḃ	Ċ	Ḋ	Ė	Ḟ	Ġ		İ				Ṁ			Ṗ			.
!												¶		§																											¶			!
?																																												?
:																																												:
;									¡																																			;
<			č	ď	ě							ľ		ň			ř	š	ť						ž			Č	Ď	Ě							Ľ		Ň				Ř	<
=			€	đ	€															¥								€	€								£		₦					=
>	â				ê				î						ô					û						Â				Ê				Î						Ô				>
-	Ā			đ	ē				ī			£			ō				ŧ	ū				¥		Ā			Đ	Ē				Ī			£			Ō				-
+																																												+
*	å																			ů						Å																		*
(	ă						ğ																			Ă						Ğ												(
)																																												)
|			¢																									¢																|
⊔																																												⊔
#																																												#
%																																												%
a	å	ă	ã												å																													a
b																																												b
c			č												©																									©				c
d			ď																																									d
e	æ		ě	ě	ə										œ																													e
f				ff																																								f
g	ğ		ǧ							ŋ																																		g
h			ħ	ð														þ																										h
i	ĭ		ǐ	⊘	fi																												ffi											i
j			ǰ					ij																									IJ											j
k			ǩ								ĸ																																	k
l			ľ	fl															|														ffl											l
m														℠	™																													m
n			ň																																									n
o	ŏ		ǒ												°	§							¤					©												№				o
p																																												p
r			ř												®													₡	Ƒ											®				r
s			š	ſ											§	ß																											Rs	s
↳	a	b	c	d	e	f	g	h	i	j	k	l	m	n	o	p	r	s	t	u	v	w	x	y	z	A	B	C	D	E	F	G	H	I	J	K	L	M	N	O	P	Q	R	↳

3.2 Compose Sequence Matrix (top right)

⏎	S	T	U	V	W	X	Y	Z	'	`	"	^	_	~	/	,	.	!	?	:	;	<	=	>	−	+	*	(	)	|	⌴	#	%	1	2	3	4	5	6	7	8	9	0	⏎
'	Ś		Ú			Ý	Ź	´			¨		!				,						‘	’									'													'
`			Ù																				`																						`
"			Ü			Ÿ			¨								„						“	”									"												"
^			Û	Ŵ	Ŷ						¯		|		·	·!									−			^					^		1	2	3								^
_			Ū															¿		≤	≡	≥											_												_
~			Ũ																							÷	~						~							θ					~
/		Ŧ										|			\					≮	≠	≯	≁										/											/
,	Ş	Ţ	Ų							,	„			˛									¬									˛	,											,
.	Ṡ	Ṫ					Ż						.				…			∴													.											.
!	§																	¡	¿													!												!
?																		?	¿													?												?
:																				∵				÷								:												:
;																																;												;
<	Š	Ť					Ž	˘		“		≤		\	‹							«	◊									ˇ	<											<
=			₩		¥						=		ˍ	≠	•						≤	≥										=											=
>			Û					'		"		≥			›						◊	»	→			^						>											>
−		Ŧ	Ū		¥								–		⊀	¬	·			÷	←			±	{	}					~		−											−
+													+		+						±	#										+											+
*			Ů																												°	*											*
(											(		(					☹		{	[				˘							(											(
)											)		)					☺		}	]											)											)
|													⊹																			|											|
⌴								'	`		^		~			˛					˘		^	~		˘							⌴											⌴
#																															♯	#											#
%																																%											%
a		ă							á	à	ä	â	ā	ã		ą	à	ą	å		ą		â	Ā		å						a											a
b																ƀ		ƀ	ḅ				♭									b											b
c									ć			ĉ				¢	ç	ċ				č	€				¢					c											c
d																đ	ḑ	đ	ḍ			ď	đ	đ								d											d
e		ě							é	è	ë	ê	ē	ẽ		ę	è	ę	ě		ę	ě	€	ê	ē							♪	e											e
f																		ḟ					♮									f											f
g		ğ							ǵ			ĝ	ḡ			ǧ	ġ	ģ														g											g
h											ḧ	ĥ				ħ	ḩ	ḣ	ḥ													h											h
i		ĭ							í	ì	ï	î	ī	ĩ		ı	į	ı	î		į		î	ī								i											i
j												ĵ																				j											j
k									ḱ							ķ		ḵ														k											k
l									ĺ							ł	ļ	ḷ				ľ	£									l											l
m	SM	TM							ḿ							ṁ	ṁ	ṃ														m											m
n									ń	ǹ		ñ				ņ	ṅ	ṇ				ň										n											n
o		ŏ		¤					ó	ò	ö	ô	ō	õ	ø	ó	ọ	ǒ	ǫ			ő	ô	ō	ơ							%ο	o											o
p									ṕ								ṗ															p											p
r									ŕ							ŗ	ṙ	ṛ				ř										r											r
s									ś			ŝ				ş	ś	ṣ				š										s											s
⇥	S	T	U	V	W	X	Y	Z	'	`	"	^	_	~	/	,	.	!	?	:	;	<	=	>	−	+	*	(	)	|	⌴	#	%	1	2	3	4	5	6	7	8	9	0	⏎

3.3 Compose Sequence Matrix (bottom left)

↵	a	b	c	d	e	f	g	h	i	j	k	l	m	n	o	p	r	s	t	u	v	w	x	y	z	A	B	C	D	E	F	G	H	I	J	K	L	M	N	O	P	Q	R	↵
t		ť																																								Pts		t
u	ŭ	ŭ											µ		ů				ŭ																									u
v												|																																v
w															ŵ																													w
x															¤					×																				¤				x
y															ŷ																													y
z		ž																	ž																									z
A	Ă	Ă													Å													Å												Ⓐ				A
B																																												B
C		Č													©																									©				C
D		Ď																																										D
E	Ě	Ě																															Æ	Œ						Œ				E
F																																												F
G	Ğ	Ğ																																				Ŋ						G
H		Ħ																										Đ																H
I	Ĭ	Ĭ																																										I
J																																		IJ										J
K		Ķ																																										K
L		Ļ																																										L
M																	SM		TM																									M
N		Ņ																																										N
O	Ö	Ö														¤												©											№				®	O
P																																										¶		P
Q																																												Q
R		Ř													®																									®				R
S		Š		ſ																																				§				S
T		Ť																															@											T
U	Ŭ	Ŭ			ğ										Ů																Ğ													U
V																																				|								V
W																																												W
X															¤																									¤				X
Y																																												Y
Z		Ž																	Ž																									Z
1																																												1
2																																												2
3																																												3
4																																												4
5																																												5
6																																												6
7																																												7
8																																												8
9																																												9
0																																												0
↵	a	b	c	d	e	f	g	h	i	j	k	l	m	n	o	p	r	s	t	u	v	w	x	y	z	A	B	C	D	E	F	G	H	I	J	K	L	M	N	O	P	Q	R	↵

3.4   Compose Sequence Matrix (bottom right)

↩	S	T	U	V	W	X	Y	Z	'	`	"	^	_	~	/	,	.	!	?	:	;	<	=	>	-	+	*	(	)	|	⎵	#	%	1	2	3	4	5	6	7	8	9	0	↩
t												ẗ						ŧ	ţ		ț			ť																					t
u		ŭ							ú	ù	ü	û	ū	ũ	µ	ų			ų	ů		ų			ű	û	ū	ư	ů																u
v									v́					ṽ	√		ʋ																												v
w									ẃ	ẁ	ẅ	ŵ					ẇ		ẉ																									w
x												ẋ							x̣																										x
y									ý	ỳ	ÿ	ŷ	ȳ	ỹ					ẏ	y̨	ẙ				¥		¥																	y
z									ź			ẑ			z	ż			ẓ					ž																				z
A		Ă							Á	À	Ä	Â	Ā	Ã		Ą	Ȧ		Ą	Å		Ą			Â	Ā		Å																A
B																	Ḃ		Ḅ																									B
C									Ć			Ĉ			¢	Ç	Ċ							Č	€			¢																C
D															Đ	Ḑ	Ḋ		Ḍ					Ď			Đ																	D
E		Ĕ							É	È	Ë	Ê	Ē	Ẽ		Ę	Ė		Ę	Ė		Ę		Ě	€	Ê	Ē						♪										E
F																	Ḟ																											F
G		Ğ							Ǵ			Ĝ	Ḡ			Ģ	Ġ																											G
H		Þ									Ḧ	Ĥ			Ħ	Ḩ	Ḣ		Ḥ																									H
I		Ĭ							Í	Ì	Ï	Î	Ī	Ĩ	Ɨ	Į	İ		Į		Į				Î	Ī																		I
J												Ĵ																																J
K									Ḱ									Ķ		Ḳ																								K
L				ǀ					Ĺ						Ł	Ļ			Ḷ					Ľ	£		£																	L
M	SM	TM							Ḿ								Ṁ		Ṃ																									M
N									Ń	Ǹ				Ñ		Ņ	Ṅ		Ṇ					Ň	Ŋ																			N
O	§	Ŏ		¤					Ó	Ò	Ö	Ô	Ō	Õ	Ø		Ȯ		Ọ	Ǫ		Ǫ			Ő	Ô	Ō	Ơ																O
P									Ṕ								Ṗ																											P
Q																																												Q
R									Ŕ							Ŗ	Ṙ		Ṛ					Ř																				R
S	ß								Ś			Ŝ				Ş	Ṡ		Ṣ					Š									♫											S
T															Ŧ	Ţ	Ṫ		Ṭ					Ť																				T
U		Ŭ							Ú	Ù	Ü	Û	Ū	Ũ		Ų			Ų	Ů		Ų			Ű	Û	Ū	Ư	Ů															U
V														Ṽ					Ṿ																									V
W									Ẃ	Ẁ	Ẅ	Ŵ					Ẇ		Ẉ						₩																			W
X												Ẍ							Ẋ																									X
Y									Ý	Ỳ	Ÿ	Ŷ	Ȳ	Ỹ					Ẏ	Ỵ	Y̊				¥		¥																	Y
Z									Ź			Ẑ			Z	Ż			Ẓ					Ž																				Z
1													¹	₁																															1
2													²	₂																						½									2
3													³	₃										♥											⅓	⅔								3
4													⁴	₄																					¼		¾							4
5													⁵	₅																				⅕	⅖	⅗	⅘						5
6													⁶	₆																				⅙				⅚					6
7													⁷	₇																				⅐									7
8													⁸	₈																				⅛		⅜		⅝		⅞	∞		8
9													⁹	₉																				⅑									9
0													⁰	₀	θ										°																			0
↩	S	T	U	V	W	X	Y	Z	'	`	"	^	_	~	/	,	.	!	?	:	;	<	=	>	-	+	*	(	)	|	⎵	#	%	1	2	3	4	5	6	7	8	9	0	↩

Chapter 4
ASCII Compose Sequences Lookup

This chapter offers an overview for looking up resulting Unicode characters for two-key, three-key and four-key compose sequences. These compose sequences are relatively easy to remember and can be created with keys found on most QWERTY-like keyboards

The keys specifically needed to enter these sequences are also the first 95 printable characters of Unicode. That is, the keys representing lower and upper case letters of the Latin alphabet a to Z, numerals 0 to 9, mathematical symbols such as + and = and punctuation marks such as ? and ". This range is identical to all of the printable ASCII characters which were in use at the time most QWERTY-like keyboards were first designed.

When for example the overview lists aa → å the following is meant by it. When pressing, and releasing, the compose key followed by pressing the key for a twice, or in other words Δ a a, the character å will be entered. In order to prevent ambiguity the Unicode identifier for the resulting character is included in the overview.

The sequences are ordered alphabetically and grouped per the first character of the sequence. Note that ␣ is used to represent the space bar ⬚. Each Unicode character is shown in the serif font from of the GNU FreeFont family.

Please consult the X.Org developers community by means of their mailing list at http://lists.x.org/mailman/listinfo/xorg-devel prior to starting any work on libX11 compose key sequences because of certain conventions and possible complex interdependencies. Monitor http://cgit.freedesktop.org/xorg/lib/libX11/log/nls/en_US.UTF-8/Compose.pre to remain up to date with the latest developments regarding these compose key sequences.

a

aa	→ å	U00E5
ae	→ æ	U00E6
a'	→ á	U00E1
a`	→ à	U00E0
a"	→ ä	U00E4
a^	→ â	U00E2
a_	→ ā	U0101
a~	→ ã	U00E3
a,	→ ą	U0105
a>	→ â	U00E2
a-	→ Ā	U0100
a*	→ å	U00E5
a(	→ ă	U0103

b

ba	→ ă	U0103
be	→ ĕ	U0115
bg	→ ğ	U011F
bi	→ ĭ	U012D
bo	→ ŏ	U014F
bu	→ ŭ	U016D
bA	→ Ă	U0102
bE	→ Ĕ	U0114
bG	→ Ğ	U011E
bI	→ Ĭ	U012C
bO	→ Ŏ	U014E
bU	→ Ŭ	U016C
b,e	→ ȩ	U1E1D
b,E	→ Ȩ	U1E1C
b.	→ ḃ	U1E03
b!a	→ ặ	U1EB7
b!A	→ Ặ	U1EB6

c

ca	→ ǎ	U01CE
cc	→ č	U010D
cd	→ ď	U010F
ce	→ ě	U011B
cg	→ ǧ	U01E7
ch	→ ȟ	U021F
ci	→ ǐ	U01D0
cj	→ ǰ	U01F0
ck	→ ǩ	U01E9
cl	→ ľ	U013E
cn	→ ň	U0148
co	→ ǒ	U01D2
cr	→ ř	U0159
cs	→ š	U0161
ct	→ ť	U0165
cu	→ ǔ	U01D4
cz	→ ž	U017E

cA	→ Ǎ	U01CD
cC	→ Č	U010C
cD	→ Ď	U010E
cE	→ Ě	U011A
cG	→ Ǧ	U01E6
cH	→ Ȟ	U021E
cI	→ Ǐ	U01CF
cK	→ Ǩ	U01E8
cL	→ Ľ	U013D
cN	→ Ň	U0147
cO	→ Ǒ	U01D1
cR	→ Ř	U0158
cS	→ Š	U0160
cT	→ Ť	U0164
cU	→ Ǔ	U01D3
cZ	→ Ž	U017D
c'	→ ć	U0107
c"u	→ ǚ	U01DA
c"U	→ Ǚ	U01D9
c/	→ ¢	U00A2
c,	→ ç	U00E7
c.	→ ċ	U010B
c<	→ č	U010D
c=	→ €	U20AC
c|	→ ¢	U00A2

d

dh	→ ð	U00F0
di	→ ∅	U2300
d,	→ ḑ	U1E11
d.	→ ḋ	U1E0B
d<	→ ď	U010F
d=	→ ₫	U20AB
d-	→ đ	U0111

e

ee	→ ə	U0259
e'	→ é	U00E9
e`	→ è	U00E8
e"	→ ë	U00EB
e^	→ ê	U00EA
e_	→ ē	U0113
e,	→ ę	U0119
e.	→ ė	U0117
e<	→ ě	U011B
e=	→ €	U20AC
e>	→ ê	U00EA
e-	→ ē	U0113

f

ff	→ ﬀ	UFB00
fi	→ ﬁ	UFB01

fl	→ ﬂ	UFB02
fs	→ ſ	U017F
fS	→ ſ	U017F
f.	→ ḟ	U1E1F

g

gU	→ ğ	U011F
g,	→ ġ	U0123
g.	→ ġ	U0121
g(	→ ğ	U011F

h

h,	→ ḩ	U1E29

i

ij	→ ĳ	U0133
i'	→ í	U00ED
i`	→ ì	U00EC
i"	→ ï	U00EF
i^	→ î	U00EE
i_	→ ī	U012B
i~	→ ĩ	U0129
i,	→ į	U012F
i.	→ ı	U0131
i;	→ į	U012F
i>	→ î	U00EE
i-	→ ī	U012B

k

kk	→ ĸ	U0138
k,	→ ķ	U0137

l

lv	→ l	U007C
l'	→ Ĺ	U013A
l/	→ ł	U0142
l,	→ ļ	U013C
l<	→ ľ	U013E
l-	→ £	U00A3

m

mu	→ µ	U00B5
m/	→ ₥	U20A5
m.	→ ṁ	U1E41

n

ng	→ ŋ	U014B
n'	→ ń	U0144
n~	→ ñ	U00F1
n,	→ ņ	U0146
n<	→ ň	U0148

o

oa	→	å	U00E5
oc	→	©	U00A9
oe	→	œ	U0153
oo	→	°	U00B0
or	→	®	U00AE
os	→	§	U00A7
ou	→	ů	U016F
ow	→	ẘ	U1E98
ox	→	¤	U00A4
oy	→	ẙ	U1E99
oA	→	Å	U00C5
oC	→	©	U00A9
oR	→	®	U00AE
oU	→	Ů	U016E
oX	→	¤	U00A4
o'	→	ó	U00F3
o`	→	ò	U00F2
o"	→	ö	U00F6
o^	→	ô	U00F4
o_	→	ō	U014D
o~	→	õ	U00F5
o/	→	ø	U00F8
o>	→	ô	U00F4
o-	→	ō	U014D

p

p.	→	ṗ	U1E57
p!	→	¶	U00B6

r

r'	→	ŕ	U0155
r,	→	ŗ	U0157
r<	→	ř	U0159

s

sm	→	℠	U2120
so	→	§	U00A7
ss	→	ß	U00DF
sM	→	℠	U2120
s'	→	ś	U015B
s,	→	ş	U015F
s.	→	ṡ	U1E61
s!	→	§	U00A7
s<	→	š	U0161

t

th	→	þ	U00FE
tm	→	™	U2122
tM	→	™	U2122
t/	→	ŧ	U0167
t,	→	ţ	U0163

t.	→	ṫ	U1E6B
t<	→	ť	U0165
t-	→	ŧ	U0167

u

uu	→	ŭ	U016D
u'	→	ú	U00FA
u`	→	ù	U00F9
u"	→	ü	U00FC
u^	→	û	U00FB
u_	→	ū	U016B
u~	→	ũ	U0169
u/	→	µ	U00B5
u,	→	ų	U0173
u>	→	û	U00FB
u-	→	ū	U016B
u*	→	ů	U016F

v

vl	→	|	U007C
vz	→	ž	U017E
vZ	→	Ž	U017D
v/	→	√	U221A

w

w^	→	ŵ	U0175

x

xo	→	¤	U00A4
xx	→	×	U00D7
xO	→	¤	U00A4

y

y'	→	ý	U00FD
y"	→	ÿ	U00FF
y^	→	ŷ	U0177
y=	→	¥	U00A5
y-	→	¥	U00A5

z

z'	→	ź	U017A
z.	→	ż	U017C
z<	→	ž	U017E

A

AA	→	Å	U00C5
AE	→	Æ	U00C6
AT	→	@	U0040
A'	→	Á	U00C1
A`	→	À	U00C0
A"	→	Ä	U00C4
A^	→	Â	U00C2

A_	→	Ā	U0100
A~	→	Ã	U00C3
A,	→	Ą	U0104
A>	→	Â	U00C2
A-	→	Ā	U0100
A*	→	Å	U00C5
A(	→	Ă	U0102

B

B.	→	Ḃ	U1E02

C

Co	→	©	U00A9
Cr	→	₢	U20A2
CCCP	→	☭	U262D
CE	→	₠	U20A0
CO	→	©	U00A9
C'	→	Ć	U0106
C/	→	₡	U20A1
C,	→	Ç	U00C7
C.	→	Ċ	U010A
C<	→	Č	U010C
C=	→	€	U20AC
C|	→	¢	U00A2

D

DH	→	Ð	U00D0
D,	→	Ḑ	U1E10
D.	→	Ḋ	U1E0A
D<	→	Ď	U010E
D-	→	Đ	U0110

E

E'	→	É	U00C9
E`	→	È	U00C8
E"	→	Ë	U00CB
E^	→	Ê	U00CA
E_	→	Ē	U0112
E,	→	Ę	U0118
E.	→	Ė	U0116
E<	→	Ě	U011A
E=	→	€	U20AC
E>	→	Ê	U00CA
E-	→	Ē	U0112

F

Fi	→	ﬃ	UFB03
Fl	→	ﬄ	UFB04
Fr	→	₣	U20A3
F.	→	Ḟ	U1E1E

G

GU	→	Ğ	U011E
G,	→	Ģ	U0122
G.	→	Ġ	U0120
G(	→	Ğ	U011E

H

H,	→	Ḩ	U1E28

I

Ij	→	IJ	U0132
IJ	→	IJ	U0132
I'	→	Í	U00CD
I`	→	Ì	U00CC
I"	→	Ï	U00CF
I^	→	Î	U00CE
I_	→	Ī	U012A
I~	→	Ĩ	U0128
I,	→	Į	U012E
I.	→	İ	U0130
I>	→	Î	U00CE
I-	→	Ī	U012A

K

K,	→	Ķ	U0136

L

LV	→	ǀ	U007C
L'	→	Ĺ	U0139
L/	→	Ł	U0141
L,	→	Ļ	U013B
L<	→	Ľ	U013D
L=	→	₤	U20A4
L-	→	£	U00A3

M

M.	→	Ṁ	U1E40

N

No	→	№	U2116
NG	→	Ŋ	U014A
NO	→	№	U2116
N'	→	Ń	U0143
N~	→	Ñ	U00D1
N,	→	Ņ	U0145
N<	→	Ň	U0147
N=	→	₦	U20A6

O

Oc	→	©	U00A9
Or	→	®	U00AE
Ox	→	¤	U00A4

OA	→	Ⓐ	U24B6
OC	→	©	U00A9
OE	→	Œ	U0152
OR	→	®	U00AE
OS	→	§	U00A7
OX	→	¤	U00A4
O'	→	Ó	U00D3
O`	→	Ò	U00D2
O"	→	Ö	U00D6
O^	→	Ô	U00D4
O_	→	Ō	U014C
O~	→	Õ	U00D5
O/	→	Ø	U00D8
O>	→	Ô	U00D4
O-	→	Ō	U014C

P

Pt	→	Pts	U20A7
PP	→	¶	U00B6
P.	→	Ṗ	U1E56
P!	→	¶	U00B6

R

Rs	→	Rs	U20A8
RO	→	®	U00AE
R'	→	Ŕ	U0154
R,	→	Ŗ	U0156
R<	→	Ř	U0158

S

Sm	→	SM	U2120
SM	→	SM	U2120
SO	→	§	U00A7
SS	→	ẞ	U1E9E
S'	→	Ś	U015A
S,	→	Ş	U015E
S.	→	Ṡ	U1E60
S!	→	§	U00A7
S<	→	Š	U0160

T

Tm	→	TM	U2122
TH	→	Þ	U00DE
TM	→	TM	U2122
T/	→	Ŧ	U0166
T,	→	Ţ	U0162
T.	→	Ṫ	U1E6A
T<	→	Ť	U0164
T-	→	Ŧ	U0166

U

Ua	→	ă	U0103

Ue	→	ĕ	U0115
Ug	→	ğ	U011F
Ui	→	ĭ	U012D
Uo	→	ŏ	U014F
Uu	→	ŭ	U016D
UA	→	Ă	U0102
UE	→	Ĕ	U0114
UG	→	Ğ	U011E
UI	→	Ĭ	U012C
UO	→	Ŏ	U014E
UU	→	Ŭ	U016C
U'	→	Ú	U00DA
U`	→	Ù	U00D9
U"	→	Ü	U00DC
U^	→	Û	U00DB
U_	→	Ū	U016A
U~	→	Ũ	U0168
U,	→	Ų	U0172
U!a	→	ặ	U1EB7
U!A	→	Ặ	U1EB6
U>	→	Û	U00DB
U-	→	Ū	U016A
U*	→	Ů	U016E
U⎵,e	→	ệ	U1E1D
U⎵,E	→	Ệ	U1E1C

V

VL	→	ǀ	U007C

W

W^	→	Ŵ	U0174
W=	→	₩	U20A9

X

Xo	→	¤	U00A4
XO	→	¤	U00A4

Y

Y'	→	Ý	U00DD
Y"	→	Ÿ	U0178
Y^	→	Ŷ	U0176
Y=	→	¥	U00A5
Y-	→	¥	U00A5

Z

Z'	→	Ź	U0179
Z.	→	Ż	U017B
Z<	→	Ž	U017D

'

'a	→	á	U00E1
'ba	→	ắ	U1EAF

'bA	→	Ắ	U1EAE	'~o	→	ố	U1E4D	"		
'c	→	ć	U0107	'~u	→	ứ	U1E79	"a	→ ä	U00E4
'e	→	é	U00E9	'~O	→	Ố	U1E4C	"e	→ ë	U00EB
'g	→	ǵ	U01F5	'~U	→	Ứ	U1E78	"h	→ ḧ	U1E27
'i	→	í	U00ED	'/o	→	ǿ	U01FF	"i	→ ï	U00EF
'k	→	ḱ	U1E31	'/O	→	Ǿ	U01FE	"o	→ ö	U00F6
'l	→	ĺ	U013A	',	→	‚	U201A	"t	→ ẗ	U1E97
'm	→	ḿ	U1E3F	'<	→	'	U2018	"u	→ ü	U00FC
'n	→	ń	U0144	'>	→	'	U2019	"w	→ ẅ	U1E85
'o	→	ó	U00F3	'+o	→	ớ	U1EDB	"x	→ ẍ	U1E8D
'p	→	ṕ	U1E55	'+u	→	ứ	U1EE9	"y	→ ÿ	U00FF
'r	→	ŕ	U0155	'+O	→	Ớ	U1EDA	"A	→ Ä	U00C4
's	→	ś	U015B	'+U	→	Ứ	U1EE8	"E	→ Ë	U00CB
'u	→	ú	U00FA	'␣	→	'	U0027	"H	→ Ḧ	U1E26
'v	→	ḱ	U045C					"I	→ Ï	U00CF
'w	→	ẃ	U1E83					"O	→ Ö	U00D6
'y	→	ý	U00FD	`				"U	→ Ü	U00DC
'z	→	ź	U017A	`a	→	à	U00E0	"W	→ Ẅ	U1E84
'A	→	Á	U00C1	`ba	→	ằ	U1EB1	"X	→ Ẍ	U1E8C
'C	→	Ć	U0106	`bA	→	Ằ	U1EB0	"Y	→ Ÿ	U0178
'E	→	É	U00C9	`e	→	è	U00E8	"'	→	̈́	U0344
'G	→	Ǵ	U01F4	`i	→	ì	U00EC	""	→	̈	U00A8
'I	→	Í	U00CD	`n	→	ǹ	U01F9	"_u	→ ṻ	U1E7B
'K	→	Ḱ	U1E30	`o	→	ò	U00F2	"_U	→ Ṻ	U1E7A
'L	→	Ĺ	U0139	`u	→	ù	U00F9	"~o	→ ȫ	U1E4F
'M	→	Ḿ	U1E3E	`w	→	ẁ	U1E81	"~O	→ Ȫ	U1E4E
'N	→	Ń	U0143	`y	→	ỳ	U1EF3	",	→ „	U201E
'O	→	Ó	U00D3	`A	→	À	U00C0	"<	→ "	U201C
'P	→	Ṕ	U1E54	`E	→	È	U00C8	">	→ "	U201D
'R	→	Ŕ	U0154	`I	→	Ì	U00CC			
'S	→	Ś	U015A	`N	→	Ǹ	U01F8	^		
'U	→	Ú	U00DA	`O	→	Ò	U00D2	^a	→ â	U00E2
'W	→	Ẃ	U1E82	`U	→	Ù	U00D9	^c	→ ĉ	U0109
'Y	→	Ý	U00DD	`W	→	Ẁ	U1E80	^e	→ ê	U00EA
'Z	→	Ź	U0179	`Y	→	Ỳ	U1EF2	^g	→ ĝ	U011D
''	→	´	U00B4	`"u	→	ǜ	U01DC	^h	→ ĥ	U0125
'"i	→	ḯ	U1E2F	`"U	→	Ǜ	U01DB	^i	→ î	U00EE
'"u	→	ǘ	U01D8	`^a	→	ầ	U1EA7	^j	→ ĵ	U0135
'"I	→	Ḯ	U1E2E	`^e	→	ề	U1EC1	^o	→ ô	U00F4
'"U	→	Ǘ	U01D7	`^o	→	ồ	U1ED3	^s	→ ŝ	U015D
'"␣	→	΅	U0385	`^A	→	Ầ	U1EA6	^u	→ û	U00FB
'^a	→	ấ	U1EA5	`^E	→	Ề	U1EC0	^w	→ ŵ	U0175
'^e	→	ế	U1EBF	`^O	→	Ồ	U1ED2	^y	→ ŷ	U0177
'^o	→	ố	U1ED1	`_e	→	ḕ	U1E15	^z	→ ẑ	U1E91
'^A	→	Ấ	U1EA4	`_o	→	ṑ	U1E51	^A	→ Â	U00C2
'^E	→	Ế	U1EBE	`_E	→	Ḕ	U1E14	^C	→ Ĉ	U0108
'^O	→	Ố	U1ED0	`_O	→	Ṑ	U1E50	^E	→ Ê	U00CA
'_e	→	ḗ	U1E17	`+o	→	ờ	U1EDD	^G	→ Ĝ	U011C
'_o	→	ṓ	U1E53	`+u	→	ừ	U1EEB	^H	→ Ĥ	U0124
'_E	→	Ḗ	U1E16	`+O	→	Ờ	U1EDC	^I	→ Î	U00CE
'_O	→	Ṓ	U1E52	`+U	→	Ừ	U1EEA	^J	→ Ĵ	U0134
				`␣	→	`	U0060	^O	→ Ô	U00D4

Seq		Char	Code
^S	→	Ŝ	U015C
^U	→	Û	U00DB
^W	→	Ŵ	U0174
^Y	→	Ŷ	U0176
^Z	→	Ẑ	U1E90
^_a	→	ᵃ	U00AA
^_h	→	ʰ	U02B0
^_i	→	ⁱ	U2071
^_j	→	ʲ	U02B2
^_l	→	ˡ	U02E1
^_n	→	ⁿ	U207F
^_o	→	º	U00BA
^_r	→	ʳ	U02B3
^_s	→	ˢ	U02E2
^_w	→	ʷ	U02B7
^_x	→	ˣ	U02E3
^_y	→	ʸ	U02B8
^/	→	|	U007C
^.	→	·	U00B7
^!a	→	ậ	U1EAD
^!e	→	ệ	U1EC7
^!o	→	ộ	U1ED9
^!A	→	Ậ	U1EAC
^!E	→	Ệ	U1EC6
^!O	→	Ộ	U1ED8
^=	→	⁼	U207C
^-	→	¯	U00AF
^+	→	⁺	U207A
^(	→	⁽	U207D
^)	→	⁾	U207E
^␣	→	^	U005E
^1	→	¹	U00B9
^2	→	²	U00B2
^3	→	³	U00B3
^4	→	⁴	U2074
^5	→	⁵	U2075
^6	→	⁶	U2076
^7	→	⁷	U2077
^8	→	⁸	U2078
^9	→	⁹	U2079
^0	→	⁰	U2070

-

Seq		Char	Code
_a	→	ā	U0101
_e	→	ē	U0113
_g	→	ḡ	U1E21
_i	→	ī	U012B
_o	→	ō	U014D
_u	→	ū	U016B
_y	→	ȳ	U0233
_A	→	Ā	U0100
_E	→	Ē	U0112
_G	→	Ḡ	U1E20
_I	→	Ī	U012A
_O	→	Ō	U014C
_U	→	Ū	U016A
_Y	→	Ȳ	U0232
_'	→	⍘	U2358
_"a	→	ǟ	U01DF
_"o	→	ȫ	U022B
_"u	→	ǖ	U01D6
_"A	→	Ǟ	U01DE
_"O	→	Ȫ	U022A
_"U	→	Ǖ	U01D5
_^	→	¯	U00AF
__	→	¯	U00AF
_~o	→	ȭ	U022D
_~O	→	Ȭ	U022C
_.a	→	ạ	U01E1
_.o	→	ọ	U0231
_.A	→	Ạ	U01E0
_.O	→	Ọ	U0230
_!l	→	ḹ	U1E39
_!r	→	ṝ	U1E5D
_!L	→	Ḹ	U1E38
_!R	→	Ṝ	U1E5C
_;o	→	ǭ	U01ED
_;O	→	Ǭ	U01EC
_<	→	≤	U2264
_=	→	₌	U208C
_>	→	≥	U2265
_+	→	₊	U208A
_(	→	₍	U208D
_)	→	₎	U208E
_1	→	₁	U2081
_2	→	₂	U2082
_3	→	₃	U2083
_4	→	₄	U2084
_5	→	₅	U2085
_6	→	₆	U2086
_7	→	₇	U2087
_8	→	₈	U2088
_9	→	₉	U2089
_0	→	₀	U2080

~

Seq		Char	Code
~a	→	ã	U00E3
~ba	→	ẵ	U1EB5
~bA	→	Ẵ	U1EB4
~e	→	ẽ	U1EBD
~i	→	ĩ	U0129
~n	→	ñ	U00F1
~o	→	õ	U00F5
~u	→	ũ	U0169
~v	→	ṽ	U1E7D
~y	→	ỹ	U1EF9
~A	→	Ã	U00C3
~E	→	Ẽ	U1EBC
~I	→	Ĩ	U0128
~N	→	Ñ	U00D1
~O	→	Õ	U00D5
~U	→	Ũ	U0168
~V	→	Ṽ	U1E7C
~Y	→	Ỹ	U1EF8
~^a	→	ẫ	U1EAB
~^e	→	ễ	U1EC5
~^o	→	ỗ	U1ED7
~^A	→	Ẫ	U1EAA
~^E	→	Ễ	U1EC4
~^O	→	Ỗ	U1ED6
~+o	→	ỡ	U1EE1
~+u	→	ữ	U1EEF
~+O	→	Ỡ	U1EE0
~+U	→	Ữ	U1EEE
~|	→	⍭	U236D
~␣	→	~	U007E
~0	→	⍬	U236C

/

Seq		Char	Code
/b	→	ƀ	U0180
/c	→	¢	U00A2
/d	→	đ	U0111
/g	→	ǥ	U01E5
/h	→	ħ	U0127
/i	→	ɨ	U0268
/l	→	ł	U0142
/m	→	₥	U20A5
/o	→	ø	U00F8
/t	→	ŧ	U0167
/u	→	µ	U00B5
/v	→	√	U221A
/z	→	ƶ	U01B6
/C	→	₡	U20A1
/D	→	Đ	U0110
/G	→	Ǥ	U01E4
/H	→	Ħ	U0126
/I	→	Ɨ	U0197
/L	→	Ł	U0141
/O	→	Ø	U00D8
/T	→	Ŧ	U0166
/Z	→	Ƶ	U01B5
/^	→	|	U007C
//	→	\	U005C
/<	→	\	U005C
/=	→	≠	U2260
/-	→	⌿	U233F

,

,a	→	ą	U0105
,c	→	ç	U00E7
,d	→	ḑ	U1E11
,e	→	ę	U0119
,g	→	ģ	U0123
,h	→	ḩ	U1E29
,i	→	į	U012F
,k	→	ķ	U0137
,l	→	ļ	U013C
,n	→	ņ	U0146
,r	→	ŗ	U0157
,s	→	ş	U015F
,t	→	ţ	U0163
,u	→	ų	U0173
,A	→	Ą	U0104
,C	→	Ç	U00C7
,D	→	Ḑ	U1E10
,E	→	Ę	U0118
,G	→	Ģ	U0122
,H	→	Ḩ	U1E28
,I	→	Į	U012E
,K	→	Ķ	U0136
,L	→	Ļ	U013B
,N	→	Ņ	U0145
,R	→	Ŗ	U0156
,S	→	Ş	U015E
,T	→	Ţ	U0162
,U	→	Ų	U0172
,'	→	,	U201A
,"	→	„	U201E
,,	→	¸	U00B8
,-	→	¬	U00AC
,␣	→	¸	U00B8

.

.a	→	ȧ	U0227
.b	→	ḃ	U1E03
.c	→	ċ	U010B
.d	→	ḋ	U1E0B
.e	→	ė	U0117
.f	→	ḟ	U1E1F
.g	→	ġ	U0121
.h	→	ḣ	U1E23
.i	→	ı	U0131
.m	→	ṁ	U1E41
.n	→	ṅ	U1E45
.o	→	ȯ	U022F
.p	→	ṗ	U1E57
.r	→	ṙ	U1E59
.s	→	ṡ	U1E61
.t	→	ṫ	U1E6B
.w	→	ẇ	U1E87

.x	→	ẋ	U1E8B
.y	→	ẏ	U1E8F
.z	→	ż	U017C
.A	→	Ȧ	U0226
.B	→	Ḃ	U1E02
.C	→	Ċ	U010A
.D	→	Ḋ	U1E0A
.E	→	Ė	U0116
.F	→	Ḟ	U1E1E
.G	→	Ġ	U0120
.H	→	Ḣ	U1E22
.I	→	İ	U0130
.M	→	Ṁ	U1E40
.N	→	Ṅ	U1E44
.O	→	Ȯ	U022E
.P	→	Ṗ	U1E56
.R	→	Ṙ	U1E58
.S	→	Ṡ	U1E60
.T	→	Ṫ	U1E6A
.W	→	Ẇ	U1E86
.X	→	Ẋ	U1E8A
.Y	→	Ẏ	U1E8E
.Z	→	Ż	U017B
.'s	→	ś	U1E65
.'S	→	Ś	U1E64
.^	→	·	U00B7
..	→	…	U2026
.!s	→	ṣ	U1E69
.!S	→	Ṣ	U1E68
.:	→	∵	U2235
.<	→	‹	U2039
.=	→	•	U2022
.>	→	›	U203A
.-	→	·	U00B7

!

!a	→	ạ	U1EA1
!b	→	ḅ	U1E05
!d	→	ḍ	U1E0D
!e	→	ẹ	U1EB9
!h	→	ḥ	U1E25
!i	→	ị	U1ECB
!k	→	ḳ	U1E33
!l	→	ḷ	U1E37
!m	→	ṃ	U1E43
!n	→	ṇ	U1E47
!o	→	ọ	U1ECD
!r	→	ṛ	U1E5B
!s	→	ṣ	U1E63
!t	→	ṭ	U1E6D
!u	→	ụ	U1EE5
!v	→	ṿ	U1E7F

!w	→	ẉ	U1E89
!y	→	ỵ	U1EF5
!z	→	ẓ	U1E93
!A	→	Ạ	U1EA0
!B	→	Ḅ	U1E04
!D	→	Ḍ	U1E0C
!E	→	Ẹ	U1EB8
!H	→	Ḥ	U1E24
!I	→	Ị	U1ECA
!K	→	Ḳ	U1E32
!L	→	Ḷ	U1E36
!M	→	Ṃ	U1E42
!N	→	Ṇ	U1E46
!O	→	Ọ	U1ECC
!R	→	Ṛ	U1E5A
!S	→	Ṣ	U1E62
!T	→	Ṭ	U1E6C
!U	→	Ụ	U1EE4
!V	→	Ṿ	U1E7E
!W	→	Ẉ	U1E88
!Y	→	Ỵ	U1EF4
!Z	→	Ẓ	U1E92
!^	→	¦	U00A6
!!	→	¡	U00A1
!?	→	‽	U203D
!+o	→	ợ	U1EE3
!+u	→	ự	U1EF1
!+O	→	Ợ	U1EE2
!+U	→	Ự	U1EF0

?

?a	→	ả	U1EA3
?ba	→	ẳ	U1EB3
?bA	→	Ẳ	U1EB2
?e	→	ẻ	U1EBB
?i	→	ỉ	U1EC9
?o	→	ỏ	U1ECF
?u	→	ủ	U1EE7
?y	→	ỷ	U1EF7
?A	→	Ả	U1EA2
?E	→	Ẻ	U1EBA
?I	→	Ỉ	U1EC8
?O	→	Ỏ	U1ECE
?U	→	Ủ	U1EE6
?Y	→	Ỷ	U1EF6
?^a	→	ẩ	U1EA9
?^e	→	ể	U1EC3
?^o	→	ổ	U1ED5
?^A	→	Ẩ	U1EA8
?^E	→	Ể	U1EC2
?^O	→	Ổ	U1ED4
?!	→	¿	U2E18

Seq		Char	Unicode
??	→	¿	U00BF
?+o	→	ở	U1EDF
?+u	→	ử	U1EED
?+O	→	Ở	U1EDE
?+U	→	Ử	U1EEC

:

Seq		Char	Unicode
:.	→	∴	U2234
:-	→	÷	U00F7
:(	→	☹	U2639
:)	→	☺	U263A

;

Seq		Char	Unicode
;a	→	ą	U0105
;e	→	ę	U0119
;i	→	į	U012F
;o	→	ǫ	U01EB
;u	→	ų	U0173
;A	→	Ą	U0104
;E	→	Ę	U0118
;I	→	Į	U012E
;O	→	Ǫ	U01EA
;U	→	Ų	U0172
;_	→	¿	U236E

<

Seq		Char	Unicode
<c	→	č	U010D
<d	→	ď	U010F
<e	→	ě	U011B
<l	→	ľ	U013E
<n	→	ň	U0148
<r	→	ř	U0159
<s	→	š	U0161
<t	→	ť	U0165
<z	→	ž	U017E
<C	→	Č	U010C
<D	→	Ď	U010E
<E	→	Ě	U011A
<L	→	Ľ	U013D
<N	→	Ň	U0147
<R	→	Ř	U0158
<S	→	Š	U0160
<T	→	Ť	U0164
<Z	→	Ž	U017D
<'	→	'	U2018
<"	→	"	U201C
<_	→	≤	U2264
</	→	≰	U226E
<<	→	«	U00AB
<=	→	≤	U2264
<>	→	◇	U22C4
<-	→	←	U2190

Seq		Char	Unicode
<_	→	ˇ	U02C7
<3	→	♥	U2665

=

Seq		Char	Unicode
=c	→	€	U20AC
=d	→	đ	U20AB
=e	→	€	U20AC
=o	→	ő	U0151
=u	→	ű	U0171
=y	→	¥	U00A5
=C	→	€	U20AC
=E	→	€	U20AC
=L	→	£	U20A4
=N	→	₦	U20A6
=O	→	Ő	U0150
=U	→	Ű	U0170
=W	→	₩	U20A9
=Y	→	¥	U00A5
=_	→	≡	U2261
=/	→	≠	U2260

>

Seq		Char	Unicode
>a	→	â	U00E2
>e	→	ê	U00EA
>i	→	î	U00EE
>o	→	ô	U00F4
>u	→	û	U00FB
>A	→	Â	U00C2
>E	→	Ê	U00CA
>I	→	Î	U00CE
>O	→	Ô	U00D4
>U	→	Û	U00DB
>'	→	'	U2019
>"	→	"	U201D
>_	→	≥	U2265
>/	→	≯	U226F
><	→	◇	U22C4
>=	→	≥	U2265
>>	→	»	U00BB
>_	→	^	U005E

-

Seq		Char	Unicode
-a	→	Ā	U0100
-d	→	đ	U0111
-e	→	ē	U0113
-i	→	ī	U012B
-l	→	£	U00A3
-o	→	ō	U014D
-u	→	ū	U016B
-y	→	¥	U00A5
-A	→	Ā	U0100
-D	→	Đ	U0110

Seq		Char	Unicode
-E	→	Ē	U0112
-I	→	Ī	U012A
-L	→	£	U00A3
-O	→	Ō	U014C
-U	→	Ū	U016A
-Y	→	¥	U00A5
-^	→	¯	U00AF
-/	→	≠	U233F
-,	→	¬	U00AC
-:	→	÷	U00F7
->	→	→	U2192
--.	→	–	U2013
---	→	—	U2014
--_	→	-	U00AD
-+	→	±	U00B1
-(	→	{	U007B
-)	→	}	U007D
-\	→	⊀	U2340
-_	→	~	U007E

+

Seq		Char	Unicode
+o	→	ơ	U01A1
+u	→	ư	U01B0
+O	→	Ơ	U01A0
+U	→	Ư	U01AF
+-	→	±	U00B1
++	→	#	U0023

*

Seq		Char	Unicode
*a	→	å	U00E5
*u	→	ů	U016F
*A	→	Å	U00C5
*U	→	Ů	U016E
*'a	→	ǻ	U01FB
*'A	→	Ǻ	U01FA
*0	→	°	U00B0

(

Seq		Char	Unicode
(a)	→	ⓐ	U24D0
(b)	→	ⓑ	U24D1
(c)	→	ⓒ	U24D2
(d)	→	ⓓ	U24D3
(e)	→	ⓔ	U24D4
(f)	→	ⓕ	U24D5
(g)	→	ⓖ	U24D6
(h)	→	ⓗ	U24D7
(i)	→	ⓘ	U24D8
(j)	→	ⓙ	U24D9
(k)	→	ⓚ	U24DA
(l)	→	ⓛ	U24DB
(m)	→	ⓜ	U24DC
(n)	→	ⓝ	U24DD

(o)	→	ⓞ	U24DE	(19)	→	⑲	U2472	#f	→ ♮ U266E
(p)	→	ⓟ	U24DF	(10)	→	⑩	U2469	#q	→ ♩ U2669
(q)	→	ⓠ	U24E0	(2)	→	②	U2461	#E	→ ♫ U266B
(r)	→	ⓡ	U24E1	(20)	→	⑳	U2473	#S	→ ♬ U266C
(s)	→	ⓢ	U24E2	(3)	→	③	U2462	##	→ ♯ U266F

(o) → ⓞ U24DE
(p) → ⓟ U24DF
(q) → ⓠ U24E0
(r) → ⓡ U24E1
(s) → ⓢ U24E2
(t) → ⓣ U24E3
(u) → ⓤ U24E4
(v) → ⓥ U24E5
(w) → ⓦ U24E6
(x) → ⓧ U24E7
(y) → ⓨ U24E8
(z) → ⓩ U24E9
(A) → Ⓐ U24B6
(B) → Ⓑ U24B7
(C) → Ⓒ U24B8
(D) → Ⓓ U24B9
(E) → Ⓔ U24BA
(F) → Ⓕ U24BB
(G) → Ⓖ U24BC
(H) → Ⓗ U24BD
(I) → Ⓘ U24BE
(J) → Ⓙ U24BF
(K) → Ⓚ U24C0
(L) → Ⓛ U24C1
(M) → Ⓜ U24C2
(N) → Ⓝ U24C3
(O) → Ⓞ U24C4
(P) → Ⓟ U24C5
(Q) → Ⓠ U24C6
(R) → Ⓡ U24C7
(S) → Ⓢ U24C8
(T) → Ⓣ U24C9
(U) → Ⓤ U24CA
(V) → Ⓥ U24CB
(W) → Ⓦ U24CC
(X) → Ⓧ U24CD
(Y) → Ⓨ U24CE
(Z) → Ⓩ U24CF
(- → { U007B
((→ [U005B
(␣ → ˘ U02D8
(1) → ① U2460
(11) → ⑪ U246A
(12) → ⑫ U246B
(13) → ⑬ U246C
(14) → ⑭ U246D
(15) → ⑮ U246E
(16) → ⑯ U246F
(17) → ⑰ U2470
(18) → ⑱ U2471

(19) → ⑲ U2472
(10) → ⑩ U2469
(2) → ② U2461
(20) → ⑳ U2473
(3) → ③ U2462
(4) → ④ U2463
(5) → ⑤ U2464
(6) → ⑥ U2465
(7) → ⑦ U2466
(8) → ⑧ U2467
(9) → ⑨ U2468
(0) → ⓪ U24EA

)
)- → } U007D
)) →] U005D

[
[] → ⌷ U2337

]
][→ ⌷ U2337

{
{} → ∅ U2205

|
|c → ¢ U00A2
|C → ¢ U00A2
|~ → ⍭ U236D

****
\- → ⍀ U2340

␣
␣' → ' U0027
␣` → ` U0060
␣^ → ^ U005E
␣~ → ~ U007E
␣, → ¸ U00B8
␣. →   U2008
␣< → ˇ U02C7
␣> → ^ U005E
␣- → ~ U007E
␣(→ ˘ U02D8
␣␣ →   U00A0

#
#b → ♭ U266D
#e → ♪ U266A

#f → ♮ U266E
#q → ♩ U2669
#E → ♫ U266B
#S → ♬ U266C
→ ♯ U266F

%
%o → ‰ U2030

1
1^ → ¹ U00B9
110 → ⅒ U2152
12 → ½ U00BD
13 → ⅓ U2153
14 → ¼ U00BC
15 → ⅕ U2155
16 → ⅙ U2159
17 → ⅐ U2150
18 → ⅛ U215B
19 → ⅑ U2151

2
2^ → ² U00B2
23 → ⅔ U2154
25 → ⅖ U2156

3
3^ → ³ U00B3
34 → ¾ U00BE
35 → ⅗ U2157
38 → ⅜ U215C

4
45 → ⅘ U2158

5
56 → ⅚ U215A
58 → ⅝ U215D

7
78 → ⅞ U215E

8
88 → ∞ U221E

0
0~ → θ U236C
0* → ° U00B0
03 → ↉ U2189

www.ingramcontent.com/pod-product-compliance
Lightning Source LLC
Chambersburg PA
CBHW060459060326
40689CB00020B/4582